What Is a Museum?

What Is a Museum?

Perspectives from National and International Museum Leaders

Edited by Kate Quinn and Alejandra Peña Gutiérrez

For the United States National Committee of the
International Council of Museums (ICOM-US)

ROWMAN & LITTLEFIELD
Lanham • Boulder • New York • London

Published by Rowman & Littlefield
An imprint of The Rowman & Littlefield Publishing Group, Inc.
4501 Forbes Boulevard, Suite 200, Lanham, Maryland 20706
www.rowman.com

86-90 Paul Street, London EC2A 4NE

British Library Cataloguing in Publication Information Available

Library of Congress Cataloging-in-Publication Data

Names: Peña Gutiérrez, Alejandra, editor. | Quinn, Kate (Museologist) editor. | International Council of Museums. United States National Committee, sponsoring body.
Title: What is a museum? : perspectives from national and international museum leaders / edited by Alejandra Peña Gutiérrez, Kate Quinn.
Description: Lanham, Maryland : Rowman & Littlefield, 2022. | "The United States National Committee of the International Council of Museums." | Includes bibliographical references and index.
Identifiers: LCCN 2022004003 (print) | LCCN 2022004004 (ebook) | ISBN 9781538167793 (cloth) | ISBN 9781538167809 (paperback) | ISBN 9781538167816 (ebook)
Subjects: LCSH: Museums—Philosophy.
Classification: LCC AM7 .W43 2022 (print) | LCC AM7 (ebook) | DDC 069.01—dc23/eng/20220304
LC record available at https://lccn.loc.gov/2022004003
LC ebook record available at https://lccn.loc.gov/2022004004

♾™ The paper used in this publication meets the minimum requirements of American National Standard for Information Sciences—Permanence of Paper for Printed Library Materials, ANSI/NISO Z39.48-1992.

Contents

Foreword

Alberto Garlandini

I have accepted with great pleasure the invitation to write a foreword to *What Is a Museum? Perspectives from National and International Museum Leaders*. This publication from the United States National Committee of the International Council on Museums (ICOM) is a challenging, ambitious, and needed initiative. Discussing what a museum is means discussing what the future of museums is.

As the world organization of museums and professionals, ICOM is actively debating the impact on museums of the challenges that our societies are facing: the crisis of traditional social identities, migration and inclusion, human rights and the fight against inequalities and racism, diversity and decolonization, urban regeneration, the digital revolution, sustainability and climate justice, pandemics. The chapters of ICOM-US's publication are a thorough, precious evidence of the ongoing discussion in the museum community.

Seventy-five years ago, on November 16, 1946, during the first General Conference of UNESCO, Chauncey Jerome Hamlin, chairman of the board of trustees of the Buffalo Museum of Science (United States), and George Salles, director of the Musées de France, convened the Constitutive Assembly of ICOM at the Musée du Louvre in Paris. This event gathered eminent museum directors from fifteen countries and the support of many others from all over the world. Since then, the world, the communities, and the relations between countries and peoples have changed radically. Museums, museology, and ICOM have followed as part of the global transformation.

Responding to the pressing requests of communities and authorities, museums have taken new social responsibilities and are striving for a larger role in society. Museums are relevant not only for their cultural and educational purposes, but also for their social and economic role in promoting citizens' well-being and the sustainable development of societies. The primary functions of museums are conservation, research, exhibition, and communication of heritage. Museums deal with collections as well as with tangible and intangible heritage outside their walls and the cultural landscapes that surround them. Museums are educational and communication hubs as well as places of inter-cultural dialogue, participation, and inclusion. Today's museums are institutes of reconciliation, critical thought, and pluralistic views.

Such a multivalent, social approach is not new for museums. Revisiting UNESCO's 1960 *Recommendation on Museums' Accessibility*, in 1972 UNESCO and ICOM organized the Santiago de Chile Round Table. The round table brought attention to the social role of museums and the need for a "democrati-zation of culture." Its final declaration proposed the idea of a holistic museum: a "society-serving museum" able to show visitors "their place in the world and make them aware of their problems, as individuals and as members of society." The Santiago Round Table defined the museum under a new light: an institution in close cooperation with local communities, committed to improving their development and quality of life. It highlighted the participation of communities to museum life and provided new, multidisciplinary interpretations of heritage.

In the twenty-first century museums are facing growing expectations and unprecedented challenges. The museums of tomorrow will not be the same as the museums of yesterday. Before the pandemic, the heritage sector was already undergoing a deep transformation. The pandemic has accelerated the need for change and innovation. The global crisis has exacerbated issues that have dogged museums for years, such as lack of funding, professional precarity, and technological gaps.

Beyond the mere recovery from the pandemic, museums must reinvent themselves and reimagine their future. "The Future of Museums: Recover and Reimagine" was the theme of International Museum Day in 2021. I am confident that the museum of the future is already being built. Every day mu-seum professionals are creating new connections with their communities and experimenting with innovative forms of cultural engagement and approaches to conservation.

The pandemic has dramatically increased inequalities. In a world where 41 percent of the population are not active internet users, digital illiteracy and the lack of digital infrastructures have widened disparities in access to heritage and in participation in cultural life. Participation means providing access to culture and heritage to all citizens, with no discrimination. Participation means the active involvement of citizens. Communities not only ask to be consulted or "listened to"; communities also demand to be involved in decision making, content development, and definition of priorities. Free access to culture is one of the human rights recognized by the United Nations Universal Declaration and by UNESCO's Declaration on Cultural Diversity. Access to culture is an indisputable key indicator of social equity and well-being.

The museum community is aware that fighting climate change and the loss of biodiversity is one of the ethical imperatives of our time. The climate crisis is having a devastating impact on the world's natural and cultural heritage,

Alberto Garlandini

tangible and intangible. The relations between man, the biosphere, and the geosphere are tight. The cultures of the world, the cultures of the Anthropocene are suffering because landscape, natural resources, and livability are endangered. Indigenous communities are at the forefront. Even native languages are in constant decline as a result of the climate crisis.

Museums and cultural institutions play a key role in fostering innovative solutions, amplifying the voice of environmental reformers, and involving all members of society in addressing climate change.

Museums are one of the most trusted institutions. They are in a unique position to support environmental policies, disseminate scientific information, and foster sustainable practices in their local communities.

The United Nations Sustainable Development Goals are essential in a post-pandemic recovery that aims for greener and more inclusive economies and for more resilient societies. In September 2019, ICOM's Kyoto General Assembly unanimously passed the resolution "On Sustainability and the Implementation of Agenda 2030: Transforming Our World."

With this resolution, ICOM committed to making the 2030 agenda the fundamental reference for its work over the next decade and beyond, at local, national, regional, and global levels. The ICOM Working Group on Sustainability is actively helping our organization in implementing Kyoto's resolution.

In the increasingly diversified world emerging from a health crisis of unprecedented scale, our museum community needs solid references in the face of whatever challenges may await in the future. ICOM Define, our international standing committee created in 2020, has adopted a participatory and transparent approach to the development of a new museum definition, which must be workable across the full spectrum of ICOM's membership. ICOM Define has been promoting the involvement of our committees and membership, with an open debate and total respect for diverse opinions.

In the past years I met and listened to many colleagues from highly diverse social, political, cultural, religious, administrative, and economic backgrounds. I learned that even if we speak different languages, we all share the lingua franca of museology. ICOM members do have the same vision and common values. They share a deep sense of belonging to one professional community. This common denominator must be strengthened: an updated museum definition will help unite professionals and keep museums relevant in society.

I am confident that in August 2022 ICOM Define will present ICOM's Prague general conference with a unifying new definition of museums.

I would like to highlight that global challenges call for global reflections and global responses. Networking and cooperation are indispensable. ICOM is closely collaborating with other international heritage organizations, such as the International Federation of Library Associations and Institutions (IFLA), the International Council of Archives (ICA), the International Council of

Monuments and Sites (ICOMOS), and the International Centre for the Study of the Preservation and Restoration of Cultural Property (ICCROM).

ICOM is committed to make the voice of museums heard at international governmental tables. I had the privilege to represent ICOM at several high-level meetings, such as strategic conferences organized by UNESCO, the United Nations' COP 26, the Organisation for Economic Co-operation and Development (OECD), the G7 and G20 countries, the Arab League for Education, Culture and Science Organization (ALECSO), and the European Union. ICOM participated to make sure that decision makers across the world recognize ICOM as an important international actor and integrate museums into their policies addressing heritage protection, education, sustainability, and the climate crisis. I am proud to say that the voice of museums has been heard.

ICOM's seventy-fifth anniversary will be a unique occasion to take stock of the present situation, look back at the history of our organization, and move forward toward our shared future. The times ahead are challenging, but in the past seventy-five years museums have managed to overcome some of the most unprecedented threats facing heritage since the Second World War. Thanks to this experience, we can learn and be prepared for what is to come.

ICOM calls museums to face those challenges and lead the change. With contributions by museum leaders from all over the world, ICOM-US's publication is a great step forward, a reference for all heritage professionals and a cornerstone of museology.

Alberto Garlandini

Preface

Kate Quinn

Museums around the world are in a moment of transformation. Their very existence is being questioned both within the museum field and the broader society. The impetus for this publication stems from a seemingly simple question, "What is a museum?" In September 2019, more than forty-five hundred museum professionals gathered for the International Council of Museums' (ICOM) 25th General Conference, held in Kyoto, Japan, and attempted to answer that question by voting on a new definition for a "museum." That vote did not come to pass. Conference attendees were divided with disagreements on the values expressed in the new definition and on the language used. The vote was tabled. National committees were asked to continue definition discussions with museum professionals in their own countries, with an expectation to revisit the vote at the 26th General Conference in 2022.

And then the COVID-19 pandemic brought the world to a stop. Plans to continue discussions in person shifted to digital resources. In mid-April 2020, the United States National Committee (ICOM-US) issued a digital survey to members to gain feedback on key components to be included in a new definition. The survey was circulated via the ICOM-US mailing list and social media platforms. The top ten components that respondents ranked as "key" in a new definition were:

1. education
2. exhibitions
3. promote and share knowledge and understanding
4. collections
5. conservation of objects or specimens
6. research
7. preservation of cultures

8. preservation/source of knowledge
9. accessibility
10. exploration of ideas

When asked what the most serious challenges faced by the United States in the coming decade would be, responses reflected the times, with "climate change," "inequality," "politics," "health care," "funding," "wealth disparities," and "COVID-19" leading the list. With these survey results in hand, it was decided that further discussion with our member base would be necessary.

When Alejandra and I were named cochairs of the ICOM-US programming committee, we were eager to establish new programs for our member base and to experiment with digital platforms that so many were forced to use during the pandemic. It was from here that ICOM-US's inaugural webinar series, "What Is a Museum? An Exploration in Six Parts," was born. The series brought together diverse national and international industry thought leaders to investigate how museums meet their sustainable, ethical, political, social, and cultural responsibilities in the twenty-first century. Our choice of speakers was meant to be as inclusive as possible and include the voices of non-American contributors. Launched in November 2020, one webinar was published each month, capping off with the final session presented during the annual meeting of the American Alliance of Museums in May 2021.

This publication captures the individual perspectives and group dialogue that occurred live in webinar series. Many speakers expanded their perspectives through written essays; some provided feedback in interview formats, and moderators capture the major points of discussion and issues raised in the sessions they moderated.

Part One, "What Is a Museum?" brings together ICOM-US cochair Tom Loughman with two pillars of the international museum community, Elaine Gurian and Rick West, to discuss the purpose of museums today.

Part Two: "Safe Places or Social Spaces?" explores the meaning and purpose of places that museums occupy.

Part Three: "The Function of Collecting" challenges traditional practices of acquisition and interpretation, and offers a recognition of the need for many institutions to deaccession and decolonize their collections.

These topics are expanded in Part Four: "The Whiteness of Museums," which directly addresses the societal inequities, systemic racism, and asymmetries of wealth and power present in museums around the globe.

The shared commitment and responsibility to society and the role of education in museums for the communities we serve is questioned in the chapters associated with Part Five: "Museums as Influencers."

We felt it important to address the pressing issues that ICOM-US members identified in the April 2020 survey. Morien Rees and Sarah Sutton unpack the biggest challenge facing our planet today—climate change—in Part Six: "Crisis,

Environmentalism, Sustainability, and Museums." Lisa Yun Lee addresses the role of museums in the housing and economic crisis and ongoing civil unrest.

Our publication concludes with an essay by our ICOM-US co-chair Lonnie G. Bunch III, secretary of the Smithsonian Institution, the world's largest museum, education, and research complex. His inspiring essay, "Seizing the Moment: The Evolution of the Twenty-First-Century Museum," provides guidance for the future of museums in the United States and abroad.

Like the webinar series, the publication is structured in such a way that each chapter builds on the one before. It is our hope that you read the chapters in order, but it is not necessary; each essay can stand alone and influence your understanding of the others when read in context.

So, why do museums exist? Whom do they serve? What are their goals? And what is a museum, exactly? The perspectives shared in the following pages are an attempt to answer those questions. Our overarching goal in creating it was to capture the myriad concepts expressed in reaction to creating a new definition and share them with museum professionals, new and seasoned alike.

SPECIAL THANKS

Many individuals made this publication possible, but it is only fitting to first thank the dynamic museum professionals whose words bring life to these issues: Tom Loughman, Alberto Garlandini, Elaine Gurian, Rick West, Diana Pardue, Andrés Roldán, Linda Norris, Ihor Poshyvailo, Bill Eiland, Danielle Kuijten, Anne Pasternak, Tukufu Zuberi, Lyndel King, George Abungu, Chris Bedford, Christina Woods, Kelly McKinley, Lauran Bonilla-Merchav, Bruno Brulon Soares, Alejandra Peña Gutíerrez, Lisa Sasaki, Lisa Yun Lee, Morien Rees, Sarah Sutton, and Lonnie Bunch. Thank you for your willingness to share your ideas both on screen and on page. The museum field will thrive because of your motivation to challenge it. It has been an honor to work with each of you on this project.

Thanks to our publishing partners, Charles Harmon and Erinn Slanina at Rowman & Littlefield, for their prompting and patience as we built this publication. A special thanks to Kara Pickman, without whose attention to detail, quick turnaround, and steadfast copyediting skills we would have been lost.

Seventy-five years ago, the International Council of Museums was founded by Chauncey J. Hamlin, an American who believed that museums held the power to bridge the social and political divides that the world faced in the aftermath of World War II. This publication builds on the tireless work of our predecessors, who since 1946 have aspired to make that belief a reality.

Today, the U.S. National Committee stewards those ideals and values forward. A sincere thanks to all our colleagues on the ICOM-US board, especially Kathy Dwyer Southern, Diana Pardue, Lyndell King, Rick West, and Bill Eiland, who facilitated the content development and acted as moderators and chapter authors for this project; and to Morgan Denault for her assistance.

To Alejandra Peña Gutiérrez, my admirable partner in this endeavor: I am so proud of all we accomplished during this year of incredible challenges. Thank you for thoughtful words, collaborative spirit, and your unwavering support.

To the executive director of ICOM-US, Molly Shevlin: Words cannot express how indispensable you have been to this project. Your dedication, patience, and capable management kept us all on track, and we are forever grateful.

Finally, my gratitude goes to ICOM-US cochairs Tom Loughman and Lonnie Bunch for your encouragement and confidence throughout this process. We wish this book to be a positive reflection of your strong leadership.

THE MUSEUM DEFINITIONS

CURRENT DEFINITION

A museum is a nonprofit permanent institution in the service of society and its development open to the public, which acquires, conserves, researches, communicates and exhibits the tangible and intangible heritage of humanity and its environment for the purposes of education, study and enjoyment.

—Adopted by the ICOM 22nd General Assembly in Vienna, Austria, on August 24, 2007

2019 PROPOSED NEW DEFINITION

Museums are democratising, inclusive and polyphonic spaces for critical dialogue about the pasts and the futures. Acknowledging and addressing the conflicts and challenges of the present, they hold artefacts and specimens in trust for society, safeguard diverse memories for future generations and guarantee equal rights and equal access to heritage for all people.

Museums are not for profit. They are participatory and transparent, and work in active partnership with and for diverse communities to collect, preserve, research, interpret, exhibit, and enhance understandings of the world, aiming to contribute to human dignity and social justice, global equality and planetary wellbeing.

—Proposed for vote at the 25th General Assembly in Kyoto, Japan, on September 6, 2019 (vote did not occur)

Kate Quinn

Changing [the definition] will not change who we are or you are, but it will signal a change in how we are seen.

—Lonnie G. Bunch III, September 6, 2019, Kyoto

We have to do better, and that starts with us, now. History remembers those who take risks and bring change.

—Richard West, September 2, 2019

Part One
What Is a Museum?

1

Framing the Question

Alejandra Peña Gutiérrez

For the past several years, an ongoing debate regarding the definition of museums has taken place both in the United States and globally. During the International Council of Museums (ICOM) triennial meeting in Kyoto in September 2019, its members were unable to reach agreement on a replacement of the outdated existing 2007 definition. As Eileen Gurian so correctly has stated, "the Kyoto debate is reminiscent of hundreds of years of debate," and as expected the matter was very unlikely to become settled that easily.

Inside and out the ICOM world, however, it had become evident that with their unwillingness to change, museums were refusing to enter the twenty-first century. As institutions, museums have remained centered in a Western binary concept of the world while their surroundings have been rapidly transforming. To make matters more critical, the unexpected events of the pandemic and the racial and historic reckonings that followed would force cultural institutions to push pause and rethink the essence of their existence because, as Thomas Loughman so correctly states in his essay, "apathy and nostalgia are (now) completely out of fashion."

There have been discussions about the difficulty of establishing one single definition that could be suitable for all museums around the globe. Others have also questioned, and rightly so, whether museums, in fact, should be limited by a standard shared definition. Or even further, whether some museums were already embracing the concepts of a new definition without the need for its existence.

As Rick West has mentioned regarding the proposed definition at Kyoto, museums might not be "every adjective and every noun that was used in that definition," but the idea then, as it remains today in this initial discussion, is to identify the common ground that will help establish the foundation for the traits we want museums to share moving forward.

The introductory essays in this section, by authors Eileen Gurian, Thomas Loughman, and Rick West, are meant to set the tone for future conversations in the book, where essential topics considered relevant, given the present turning point, are meant to be more deeply discussed.

The authors of this section, like all of us in the book—and hopefully many others in the museum world beyond ICOM—share some basic premises that we believe should not be ignored moving forward—that is, if we intend to remain relevant as the influential institutions we have for so many years claimed to be and don't want to risk becoming "distant in history's rearview mirror," as West so poignantly warns us in his essay.

Despite their differences, all museums seem to face similar challenges. Every respected museum today, therefore, is rethinking its purpose and mission in a search to meet the moment. To remain relevant, museums urgently need to renegotiate their role and debt to society, achieve social reconciliation, and meet their expectations for the future.

With all that has happened in the past few years, museums need to make a point of further developing a new identity. As the trusted sources of information that we have become, we need to be more dynamic, increase our topicality, and expand our ways to create awareness around many of the issues that we are facing daily and that will have a definite impact on the future of our society.

Gurian's concept of "centering," explained in her essay, reinforces the importance of people and "moves the emphasis from an equation of balance to an alternate meaning, that of hub or fulcrum from which all things flow and connect, making humans the ingredient most crucial to the museum's existence."

As cultural institutions, museums must aspire not only to achieve the involvement but also the integration of their diverse communities. A more direct participation in civic engagement and a shift of power, or using Gurian's words, "ceding power," will make it possible to attain the true inclusion and representation that we owe our communities.

We like to think of museums as influencers and agents of change. Cultural institutions often give society a sense of purpose, they can have the power to hold us together and help us adapt, but this will only abide if we remain faithful to the reflection of our times and the multiple interests of our society, acknowledging every relevant current social and political matter and considering each component of our context to reshape the future of our institutions.

Given recent events, it is hard to imagine how a wide number of these institutions might survive without the acceptance and full assumption of responsibility for their colonial origins, followed by a significant shift in their historic narrative as well as a turn in their hierarchical practices and structures.

Alejandra Peña Gutiérrez

Because this is not the first time in which the role of museums and their civic obligations have been questioned, it becomes necessary to take a deep look into the past and acknowledge our biases and shortcomings, to adopt the "new behaviors" that Gurian names and our other authors also refer to in their essays.

We would like to see fully materialize the statement that West makes in his essay when he reassures us that "the times have changed, and museum definitions need to adapt, not to the exclusion of all that has been but to the inclusion of what might also be in the future." Everything seems to point toward the fact that unlike what has happened in the past, this time society will not settle for "the promotion of the 'ethnic-specific museum,'" and those absent narratives will, in fact, begin "permeating encyclopedic museums of all typologies."

Through these initial essays we will see how many of the concepts that we consider today as "hot topics" have been a source of concern and debate for decades. Similar circumstances in the past have forced museums to question their weak interest in civic matters, as well as their lack of consideration to address the concerns of all members of society with the use of a language that speaks to all and not just a few.

Loughman's essay ends with very helpful "frank ideas" on how to "move forward on three key issues, connected to public trust," but as he also unarguably states in the beginning of his text, the dichotomy of museums could have them evolve in almost opposite directions. Loughman talks about an idealistic component that coexists with the institutional one. On a similar note, Gurian sees the museum world as composed by "the classicists who are about power, about money and about collections" and "the communitarians who are about the will of the people and their voice coming through." Whereas Loughman's idea finds its origin in the nature of the institution, Gurian's, like her work, is all about the people. The truth is that these opposite forces coexist in museums, as they do in life; and if their rationale and purpose are not seriously revisited, we could very easily end up justifying either reform or preservation of long-existing practices that we believe should undergo serious transformation.

West's words "the museum is counterpoint" and that it should "serve as a notable chink in that contemporary armor of political and social polarities and the disabling cultural and historical gloom they engender" constitute the perfect frame for why ICOM-US decided to address these matters and promote a dialogue between colleagues that can help redefine the future of museums.

The interest and participation in these conversations left us feeling that there seems to be a genuine desire for transformation in the field. Whether this comes from a solid conviction about the need for change, or just as a reaction to the recent social pressures and very justified increasing demands for transparency, is still to be determined. In any case, it will really make a difference if as a result we all agree to dismantle our authority and find together the best path ahead to be rightfully relevant to our communities.

Loughman explains to us how with more frequency purpose has had an impact on strategic planning, "from purpose, the necessary vision can be developed, the expressed mission articulated, and core values identified. Together, these aid the creation of an effective workplace and empower the museum to deliver greater impact with the communities it strives to serve." As West puts it, "this comes back to the personal exercise of normative and ethics" and the "translation of that into an institutional framework." Gurian urges every museum to "re-examine its attitudes, policies, actions, and implicit assumptions and ask a wide range of people unengaged with the museum and unrelated to each other what it is that they want and need." As our three authors for this section converge, the results of these discussions must be reflected in policies and strategic plans as means to assure the permanence of our needed transformation.

It is our hope that this time things indeed will change at their core, rather than the gradual, often reticent adaptations that we have witnessed with past demands for change. We are hopeful that museums will listen carefully and foster a necessary dialogue whose conclusions can be translated into policies that will help us attain Gurian's vision of museums as those long-yearned-for "spaces where strangers meet each other and make decisions about peace."

Alejandra Peña Gutiérrez

2

Public Trust at American Museums Today

OBSERVATIONS AND PRIORITIES

Thomas J. Loughman

Museums in the United States have long been important sites of engagement where debates about the past and future of culture, assertions of social aspirations and values, and a certain reckoning of relevance and status all play out. Sometimes these museums are sites for triumphalism and celebration, whereas at other times they can be a forum for self-doubt and mourning. Over the past five years, the museum has seen a fair share of the former and perhaps a greater share of the latter as American society has navigated an ever more contentious landscape around questions of power and voice. Perhaps this is to be expected in light of the museum community's particular mix of idealism and institutionalism.[1]

Indeed, Americans have witnessed a turbulent cascade of protest and crisis on a staggering range of serious concerns: climate change, economic stagnation, changing attitudes in philanthropy, social injustice and human rights concerns here and abroad, and shifting attitudes about and definitions of culture and its relation to objects. And so, for those seeking to shape societal attitudes at large, the museum looks like a tool for reform and a conspicuous platform for galvanizing protest. For those dedicated to preserving institutions, the museum appears to be a stabilizing force that should lead with an authentic dedication to promoting civil discourse. Apathy and nostalgia are completely out of fashion; in spite of (or rather, to spite) former president Donald Trump's homespun slogan "Make America Great Again," nary a museum of stature espoused such jingoism in its programs, collections, approach to management, or branding. Marginal, too, were nihilistic voices calling for the dissolution of museums altogether.[2]

So uniform was the desire among museum leaders toward a more socially engaged practice that it led me to see the matter differently, as a function of differing expectations of time line and mode. The question "How ought our museum formally engage the multiple crises befalling American culture?" is as complex as any. Such conundrums become more manageable when discussed within the specificity of time and means, and one flounders if left abstract and undefined. Yet the genuine and widespread desire to make our institutions matter beyond their traditional (and notably elite) circles of enthusiasts and specialists remains a hostage of the question.

A sharp cleavage—a divide over the prudent speed of, rather than need for, reform and innovation—has hampered progress at many museums in the United States. In the one camp are those who want the museum to act as an amplifying lens focused on society's problems, to give immediate visibility to grievance and injustice. In another camp are those committed to furthering the museum's role as catalyst for sustainable change over time, which puts a premium on seeking common ground and cultivating a compelling consensus among multiple stakeholders. Both groups seek to make museums more accountable to the communities they serve and genuinely aim to serve the public trust broadly.

Attending to matters of the public trust will prove invaluable at a time in which we are increasingly isolated and uncivil, off-balance and frightened, and yearning to come together. If ever there was a time for museums to set aside rivalries and transcend them, it would be the current moment. Now is the time to commit to the work ahead of reweaving cultural experiences in America equipped with a sobriety about the field's shortcomings, but also alive to the possibility that lies at the intersection of objects, people, and ideas. If we can focus our efforts on the purposeful and ecumenical engagement of art and audiences, we will be investing in our museums' capacity to be effective places for inciting curiosity, fostering self-discovery, and generating conversations about the future. For these next steps to take root will require an understanding of how America's museums were struggling before the pandemic and how those struggles coincided with a global debate about museum purpose. Finally, this essay offers frank ideas on what we should be doing to propel our institutions forward and meet the cultural needs of society today.

PURPOSE, EXPRESSED COMMUNALLY

There was once a saying that any great American city needs great museums. This optimistic, laudatory view of the role of museums catalyzed the creation of institutions of culture, famously in the nineteenth century in industrializing metropolises such as Cincinnati and Boston, but also more recently in centers of the twenty-first-century economy such as Nashville and Bentonville. In so many museums' founding stories are calls to civic action to improve society by creating and growing cultural institutions. More often than not, these new

Thomas J. Loughman

(or greatly expanded) museum entities are organized as private nonprofit corporations that solicit charitable gifts, are governed locally, and pursue their work independently. In this the American museum community differs from the global norm; institutions abroad are largely state sponsored and often state administered. This is also true of myriad other social enterprises: hospitals, higher education, human relief, and other community-focused entities are often privately administered in the public trust rather than functions of government. Museum work, therefore, has put a premium on engaging a constantly shifting group of stakeholders that ranges from the people who live and work in the immediate service area to a broad set of colleagues regionally or even globally.

Museums have worked for decades to enhance their ability to connect to the people they serve, seeking greater dialogue with stakeholders about what interests them and about how the museum can be more responsive to the public at large. Modern feedback techniques are used in American cultural institutions just as they are in other fields of social and commercial enterprise (e.g., focus groups, quantitative feedback) and form part of a system of measuring outcomes. That market data, however, requires a visible set of goals to have meaning. Setting goals is the key.

Getting to the heart of what we aspire to do through conscious consideration of common purpose has led many American institutions over the past decade to look to purpose-based organizational planning. With increasing frequency, strategic policy begins with the question of purpose. If we all can interrogate purpose and arrive at a common expression of that goal, that unity can result in a cascade of coordinated action. Clarity of purpose also allows for a modern governance model for museums in which the staff, management, and board share in the common effort of developing and monitoring impact. From purpose, the necessary vision can be developed, the expressed mission articulated, and core values identified. Together, these aid the creation of an effective workplace and empower the museum to deliver greater impact within the communities it strives to serve.

These parallels between the museum and corporate America in planning trends coincided in recent years with a parallel effort to define purpose. In the very same month in which the Business Roundtable, the high-profile association of American corporate CEOs, released a freshly composed declaration of the stakeholder-centered purpose of business,[3] a congruent conversation happening globally within the museum community about redefining the museum in purpose-centered language came to a head.

Fundamental steps in engaging the thorny question of "What is a museum?" began afresh within the International Council of Museums (ICOM) community at the time of the 2016 Triennial in Milan. A committee was established for the purpose of instigating a review of the language used to define the museum field universally in the ICOM statutes. Then, in the spring and summer of 2018, the national committees worldwide were asked to conduct interviews of professionals within the field, in which we asked four fundamental questions:

1. What do you think are the strongest trends and most serious challenges faced in your country in the coming decade?
2. What do you think are the most relevant and important contributions that museums can make to society in the coming decade?
3. What do you think are the strongest trends and most serious challenges faced by museums in your country for the coming decade?
4. How do you think museums need to change and adapt our principles, values, and working methods over the coming decade to meet those challenges and enrich our contributions?

Hundreds of museum professionals from across the United States contributed to the thousands of responses collected worldwide, which were transcribed and forwarded to our ICOM colleagues serving on the Committee for Museum Definition, Prospects and Potentials (MDPP).

On their face, the questions were intended to advance the formal and ambitious process to update the definition of museums for today. Yet this survey accomplished something far more creative. Simply put, soliciting answers to the questions invited our colleagues to engage in the bigger matter of asking, "What should museums be doing as cultural engines within society going forward?" Moreover, it took the otherwise anodyne matter of a technical definition into the territory of a purpose-driven discussion. The experience left me and the members of the ICOM-US board of directors confident in the definition process's capacity to elicit a genuine portrait of professional attitudes in the field—the community asked real questions in a spirit of openness, after all— and also optimistic that the process would yield a more modern definition to be debated and adopted at the 2019 Triennial Conference in Kyoto.

FLASHPOINTS, ABROAD AND AT HOME

We were wrong. Although historically the ICOM triennial has been the site of heated debate, the convening in Kyoto in the late summer of 2019 was exceptionally fractious. Voices for a modernized definition that ballyhooed the socially centered purpose of museums were seemingly at odds with others who wanted to reassert the more staid language now in place, with its premium on the preservation of cultural patrimony.[4]

In a world of scarcity, fear, and partisanship, compromise was not a popular option, nor did change prevail. Strident debate consumed several days and overshadowed the meetings. A failed vote at the end of the week required the definition matter to be tabled. The challenges broached in Kyoto will remain daunting for some time and are likely to be exacerbated by international struggles for authority, time line, and priorities. In early 2020, a new definition pro-

Thomas J. Loughman

cess was launched. Shortly thereafter, a governance crisis with roots in the definition debate shook ICOM's leadership corps—thought leaders from the MDPP and the executive board resigned, and ultimately so did ICOM's president, Suay Aksoy. All this occurred in the atmosphere of the then-accelerating COVID-19 pandemic and the emergency closure of nearly every cultural institution on the planet. Since mid-2020, further engagement with the general membership has pursued new language. The definition is to be considered again at the August 2022 Triennial in Prague.

Meanwhile, 2019 brought challenges to the status quo and calls for immediate redress in louder terms than had been heard in decades, adding more pressure on professional staff and governing boards. Demands for action boiled over on issues including workplace equity, an expedited push for heightened social consciousness within programming, and governance reform. Should museums accept philanthropic gifts from donors and trustees who derive their wealth from socially objectionable enterprises?[5] Could unionization not only ensure museum employees' rights but also give workers a voice in matters including how their institutions are governed and how completely they address broader issues of social equity?[6] If any mind-set defined 2019 in America's museum workplaces, it was a sense of unease and tension—a condition that would be amplified during the ensuing era of cascading social crises.

As institutions grappled with a universal and simultaneous global health crisis of terrifying virulence, they repeatedly found themselves drawn into deep social issues that have been festering for a generation. The museum world—in the jaws of COVID-19 in 2020–2021, now looking forward—has been stymied as it engages in discussions on such topics, owing in part to a divergence in expectations. Those who believe museums should be part of the cure remain frustrated and unfulfilled. Institutions and their teams labor just to get by and yearn to get back to serving the public, hampered by the specter of being called out for a misstep in the eyes of impatient and increasingly digital-based critics. Thoughtful, passionate, and articulate as the proponents in these crucial debates are, the desire to see museums at the vanguard of social change far outstrips any single institution's capacity for quick results, leading some to call for a nationwide governmental intervention in the cultural sector.[7]

PRINCIPLES FOR MOVING FORWARD

Amid this dynamic context, and regardless of how each museum chooses to proceed, it seems fundamental that we move forward on three key issues, each one connected to the public trust:

1. Staff, volunteers, and trustees must work together to define the impact they strive to make. Alignment around service to the public—near and far, those who visit habitually and those who may live a continent away—is our common responsibility and requires a joint vision. This likely means

adopting more institution-wide approaches and rethinking governance goals. Proceeding with unity of purpose and clarity of intent is essential.

2. A renewed commitment to the power of storytelling and objects will benefit from bringing in collaborating voices. Compelling stories and collections can and should elicit the curiosity and wonder of all kinds of people, in an array of modes that speak to the emotions and ideas of today. Audiences yearn for this, and the current moment demands a shift toward expanded networks of collaborators to shape the experience. Those telling the stories, the variety of perspectives that we cultivate, and the connections we make between the public and the objects are key to generating impact going forward.

3. Let's ensure that the art museum is a place for experiencing a wider range of cultures and a broader range of views. People seeking perspective and an opportunity to contemplate their own condition benefit from the remarkable array of human expression possible in our spaces. Welcome them. The public craves and deserves multiple pathways to the art of our time and the art of the past, which are inherently in constant dialogue; our changing perceptions mediate both fluidly. By championing old and new alike, the culturally immediate and the unfamiliar, our work ensures that art flourishes in the imaginations of many more than aesthetes, specialists, and artists themselves.

To move forward productively, we must recognize another public trust challenge inherent to our global reality: museums in the United States hold, display, borrow, and interpret cultural property from myriad cultures around the world. There is surely no single recipe for the nuanced and specific work of stewarding the heritage of human creativity (drawn from throughout history and the world over) in ways that appropriately resist the inclination to become the paternalistic voice for those objects. It is our responsibility to make sure that our museums approach this work respectfully and thoughtfully. Greater access to objects is a crucial step in enabling resolution of a sometimes inequitable past as we consider and develop new models of stewardship in dialogue with global partners.

We are emerging from a moment of intense trial, in which so much effort was devoted to our art museums and other cultural institutions in the hopes of preserving their future value to society. We will do well to meet the challenge with a similar level of conviction as we work to ensure that we are increasingly competent, sensitive, and responsive.

NOTES

1. See Laura Raicovich, *Culture Strike: Art and Museums in an Age of Protest* (New York: Verso, 2021).

2. See, for example, the review of Raicovich's book by former New Museum employee Dana Kopel, "Is It Time to Abolish Museums?," *Nation*, May 25, 2021, https://www.thenation.com/article/culture/culture-strike-laura-raicovich/.
3. For a summary of the debate around corporate purpose from the period, see "What Companies Are For," *Economist*, August 24, 2019.
4. See Kate Brown, "Are Art Institutions Becoming Too 'Ideological'? A Debate Breaks Out at the International Council of Museums over Politics in the Galleries," *ArtNet News*, August 20, 2019, https://news.artnet.com/art-world/icom-museum-definition-debate-1630312; Vincent Noce, "What Exactly Is a museum? ICOM Comes to Blows over New Definition," *Art Newspaper*, August 19, 2019, https://www.theartnewspaper.com/2019/08/19/what-exactly-is-a-museum-icom-comes-to-blows-over-new-definition.
5. See Julia Halperin, "In an Age of Political Division and Dirty Money, Can Museum Boards Ever Be Immaculate? Some Think They Have Found a Solution," *ArtNet News*, July 17, 2019, https://news.artnet.com/art-world/boards-museums-money-2019-1600507.
6. Catherine Wagley, "Museum Workers across the Country Are Unionizing. Here's What's Driving a Movement That's Been Years in the Making," *ArtNet News*, November 25, 2019, https://news.artnet.com/market/union-museum-analysis-1714716.
7. See Jason Farago, "The Arts Are in Crisis. Here's How Biden Can Help," *New York Times*, January 13, 2021, https://www.nytimes.com/2021/01/13/arts/design/arts-stimulus-biden.html.

3

How Do We Center People in Museums?

Elaine Heumann Gurian

The word "centering" and its root word—"center"—have had and continue to have multiple meanings in a museum context. The differing definitions are the basis of this chapter.

In October 2021, the Mid-Atlantic Association of Museums (MAAM) held a virtual conference titled "How Do We Center People in Museums?" Coincidentally, my newly published book uses the same word—"center"—in its title, *Centering the Museum: Writings for the Post-Covid Age*, and I took that occasion, as the keynote speaker of the Steven E. Weil lecture, to opine on the word and its many interrelated meanings.

Not surprisingly, I also used the occasion to include Steve Weil's thoughts on the subject, as he had been my good friend and an important museum thinker who helped shape my own ideas. Parsing the meanings of words was a lifelong focus of his. And for those who did not know him personally, Steve, in addition to being a wordsmith, was also one of the greatest joke tellers in the museum world. That was true not only because[1] he relied on the precision of a word's multiple meanings. He delighted in taking unexpected, hilarious, and abrupt sharp turns on a seemingly straight road.

THE MEANING OF "CENTER"

One of the meanings of the word is related to one of Steve's most memorable phrases, which he used as a title of a 1999 essay published in *Daedalus*: "From Being *about* Something to Being *for* Somebody" (Weil, 1999).[2] In that article, Steve suggested that museums embrace a new (at the time) museum equation: an equal sign between the museum's collection ("something") and the museum's audience ("somebody"). This usage refers to "center" as the middle point between two equal forces. The article was written at a time when this idea was advancing from the left wing of the museum community, as pushed by museum educators like me.

When Steve and I entered the museum field decades earlier (me in 1969), there was no such equation, but rather a generally held lopsided assumption that objects of importance would be presented to a passive audience by institutions of authority and power. The collection, and the museum's physical and intellectual control of it, was primary. Steve's article elevated the importance of people and their needs, and placed collection objects in their service. Since then, a readjustment of balance between objects and people has continued, albeit with uneven realization.

MAAM's conference was presented twenty-some years after Steve's article tilted the equal sign even more toward the needs of people. In the conference title, the word "center" moves the emphasis from an equation of balance to an alternate meaning, that of hub or fulcrum from which all things flow and connect, making humans the ingredient most crucial to the museum's existence.

The idea of making all aspects of the human encounter central in museums is easy to grasp, if not universally shared. Actions required to achieve such a centrality become clear in response to simple questions: How might museums address people's wants or needs? In what ways do people want to be involved with museum holdings, buildings, their many assets, and external networks of connectedness?

Of course, the reader could rightly be thinking, "Ask whom these questions?" And to that, I unhelpfully answer, "It depends." For example, when dealing with Indigenous material, I would ask the tribally acknowledged descendants of the makers about all things surrounding the object itself—where and how it is kept, what is said about it, if it can be shown, and when and whether it is to be used or returned.

And more than ask, I would clarify that, in any dispute between us, it would be the Native spokespersons who would prevail. And I know that formula certainly is not widely shared. Yet let me be clear: centering people in the museum often means ceding power. It means that by simply asking questions, the outcome becomes uncertain, regardless of the law, ownership, programmatic intention, and so on. Centering people should include determining who has standing, ultimately, to make decisions.

In today's diversity, equity, and inclusivity (DEAI) context, centering finally means that the group of people involved in decision making should always include formerly excluded relevant stakeholders. I contend that the position has seemed relatively easy to endorse—that we must diversify our staffs, boards, and advisers so that those entrusted with authority are more fully representative. And I applaud such pronouncements. But what does this really mean in practice?

In some museums, we are seeing more diversity among staff members, and the ideas that diversity brings to bear are more varied than those that come out of more homogenous staffs. But I have only occasionally seen evidence of the long-needed reformation of the human resources system, and I rarely see practices that interrogate the assumptions of recruitment itself. If we are really interested in broadening the ideas that our staff present, we need to reshape recruitment and job descriptions, which have privileged academic achievements and prior experience in similar jobs over alternate forms of expertise and training. We need to look again at our organizational structures and the centrality of the curator, making the people's representatives—however they may be called—more central. Because without a thorough review of our work assumptions, the people hired by our institutions, no matter their color, may not represent the much broader experiences of community, class, traditions, and different worldviews found in faith-based and Indigenous communities.

In simple terms, I do not yet see the kind of rethinking of the institution required to center people. To succeed in doing so, we must include expanding our definitions of work, works, and workers and think creatively about our buildings' usefulness as resources that can be made available to our neighborhoods. That could mean expanded food services, multi-activated gathering spaces, and a comprehensive view of collections' access and use. Repairing the systemic part of systemic racism requires committing to the reform of the system itself.

MY MEANING OF CENTERING

I should point out that "centering" in my book has a different but related meaning. I have come to what might be regarded as a post-radical view of our essential mission "of, by, and for all" the people, as Nina Simon would say.[3] I could now be considered a stealth conservative.

Centering the Museum is about occupying, helping to orchestrate, and celebrating an altogether different center—the political center. A definition of "political center" is the "philosophy of taking a moderate position that avoids extremes, as of right and left."[4] The political center is often derided as insufficiently principled, woefully bland, and wimpy in execution by the purists of contesting opinions. I want museums to produce less overt intellectual heat and more radical innocuousness.

In my writings, I urge museums to become explicators of complexity by modeling human compassion for uncertainty, encouraging people to come together to learn about, live uneasily with, and tolerate partial and exploratory resolutions for issues of consequence. The center, in my world, is messy and unclear, and the choices include compromises that are often logically shaky.

I wish to take modeling civility and decency seriously, so that the museum becomes a welcome, safe location for many points of view. This requires a much-expanded definition of centering, with exhibitions on one side of the equation and many other sociable activities on the other. It is the definition of "museum" itself that needs expanding.

BACKGROUND

Let me put this in context. In 2021, the world remains in a partially controlled COVID-19 pandemic, with effective vaccines unevenly available worldwide and unevenly used in the United States. The length of the quarantine, social distancing, and enhanced safety measures we have experienced have changed the meaning and location of many forms of work forever. They have also downsized our avenues for in-person gathering.

Politically, the situation in the United States now includes a president who has a more recognizably rational, focused, and workmanlike administration than did his predecessor. We have a return to overall economic well-being for many, but a chasm of left-out poor remains. Thanks to the Black Lives Matter (BLM) movement and this new administration, we have entered a society-wide debate about the responsibilities we collectively have to those excluded from the mainstream—especially, given our nation's history, Black people and people of color.

Yet many citizens seem only dimly aware that recent political upheavals are a result in part of significant disparities of income and wealth (class) and attendant restricted opportunities for the poor. Bringing the impoverished along, regardless of color, is a matter of mutual survival, not simply of good deed. Historically, profound inequality of income and power continues until the aggrieved take to the streets, not only in protest (which is hopeful) but in anger (which is not). It is precisely that anger that threatens our current democracy. And the rage arises surprisingly less so in those communities that have so long suffered and been morally wronged than in those who think recent attention to rectifying an implacable past for some has now consequently disadvantaged them. They are often the "other," the White poor. In other words, museums need to rebalance the center by adding those who have always been missing *and* by reaching out to those who now openly (and sometimes violently) express feelings of being under threat, rooted in their belief that our country is a zero-sum universe in which all BIPOC gains further diminish theirs. Although that is a racist position, acknowledging and addressing this pain without agreeing with its cause is a path neither well understood nor often approached. But it is what I am urging. I realize that reconciliation is usually a stage that follows long after violence. I suggest we short-circuit that by trying preemptive reconciliation to avert any upcoming cataclysm.

The extremists on the far-right fringe, the irrational and hateful white supremacists, put us all in danger. They align with and help promote retrograde policies that 25 to 40 percent of our U.S. electorate favor. The United States has more overtly aggrieved citizens than I understood, and they have been encouraged to act out. I am the American-born child of German-Jewish immigrants, and I grew up during the Holocaust. My people have seen this history before, and it turns out very badly.

The museum sector has a civic obligation to help resolve this festering mess. This means working among people we do not really know, often don't sympathize with, and have not taken the time to understand. We need to engage with some of those who question truth, facts, and, ultimately, democracy—and those who mostly do not use museums.

I am genuinely alarmed and have no prescriptions to offer other than dramatically expanding our current definition of "inclusion." Individually, we must advocate for all the disadvantaged—not just the communities we have unjustly ignored before. It is an "all-in" center that I am promoting. And I understand how implausible that may sound: We need to be ever more inclusive toward those we marginalized in the past *and* toward those who feel newly threatened by that inclusion? But that is precisely the task at hand.

Such expanded inclusion should not extend to the extreme fringes. I am wholeheartedly against embracing the violent edges of the political spectrum. I endorse and implore the adoption of all methods for engaging potentially reconcilable (or at least tolerant) adversaries to form a more extensive, workable—if uneasy—middle. The boundaries between such and their respective extreme fringes will likely reveal themselves by the presence or absence of civility, a related matter crucial to an enlarged center. Accordingly, I am also advocating for an overt announcement of the rules of civility within our institutions and then enforcing them. And I do not mean the august rules of upper-class etiquette and style, but simplified standards required to maintain common decency. I am for an organic, slightly unruly, messy—but civil—center, not a free-for-all.

POST-COVID-19

Having studied museum practices during the COVID-19 shutdown, I was disappointed to find that most institutions, while gradually reopening, continued to behave as if their prior methods and purposes were exemplary, and as if the only changes needed were safe social distancing methodologies, a new infusion of people of color, and more collections related to minority cultures to round out their missions.

I felt otherwise. I thought the closed-down interregnum provided a rare opportunity to reconsider first principles. And I chose "centering" to be the word that might epitomize the thoroughgoing change I was seeking. I envisioned museums as useful centers for meeting real needs and desires—a people's place that reimagines the visitor as friend, neighbor, owner, partner, and perhaps cocreator.

I had hoped a focus on people would mean more than a post-pandemic resumption of services to the already committed with an obligatory condescension toward those who had less, as was too often the case in the past. But in place of wholesale change, or at least creative experimentation, instead there has been too much reliance on mere words. The times feel almost calamitous, with an urgent need to address climate change, respond to BLM, and come to grips with resurgent white supremacy. Whatever viewpoint you hold, the methodology to begin a successful reconciliation across deeply divergent positions is not yet clear. The post-COVID-19, post-BLM, civic-minded decolonized museum is an institution whose creation continues to await our collective efforts.

Now is the time for brave approximation, exploration, and messy tryouts—not just the same institutions doing the same old things with a few new programs, exhibitions, and people added to feel sufficiently cleansed from all the unwelcome fuss and bother. My center seeks to accommodate new behaviors inside our institutions to model a society outside our walls that promotes the peaceable coexistence of irreconcilable differences.

CONCLUSION

Here is where I am landing. In this era of social upheaval, I implore museums to take the time to study and implement meaningful changes in policy and make plain that we have something of real value for those who haven't found us meaningful yet. I hope a commitment to centering people means that every museum will reexamine its attitudes, policies, actions, and implicit assumptions, and ask a wide range of people unengaged with the museum and unrelated to one another what it is that they want and need.

I encountered the same museum dis-ease late in Steve Weil's life. "Was it all for naught?" he once asked me, close to the end of his days. I reassured him that his efforts had not been in vain. I believe we have continued to do positive work, with much more remaining to be done together on a challenging and fascinating journey.

NOTES

1. This chapter contains some sentences written for the introduction in Elaine Heumann Gurian, *Centering the Museum: Writings for the Post-Covid Age* (New York: Routledge, 2021), 1–7, included here with the permission of the publisher. Taken together, these were combined with new thinking from a speech given at the Stephen E. Weil Memorial Lecture for the Mid-Atlantic Association of Museums on October 6, 2021. I thank Wendy Luke, Steve's widow, for the invitation.
2. S. Weil, "From Being About Something to Being for Somebody: The Ongoing Transformation of the American Museum," *Daedalus* 128, no. 3 (1999): 229–58.
3. Nina Simon founded the nonprofit organization OF/BY/FOR ALL that works with museum network partners to share and spread innovative practices for community-driven institutional change.
4. *American Heritage Dictionary of the English Language*, 5th ed. (2016), s.v. "centrism."

4

Museums Must Be More

ICOM'S DEFINITION OF "MUSEUM" NEEDS TO TAKE INTO ACCOUNT
HOW THE FIELD HAS CHANGED AND WHERE IT IS HEADING

W. Richard West Jr.

For the past two years in the global museum community, one issue has generated an immense volume of discussion and associated passion: whether the
definition of "museum," adopted by the International Council of Museums
(ICOM) in 2007, needs to be altered or should remain the same. The current
provision is the following:

> A museum is a non-profit, permanent institution in the service of society and
> its development, open to the public, which acquires, conserves, researches,
> communicates and exhibits the tangible and intangible heritage of humanity
> and its environment for the purposes of education, study and enjoyment.

The descendancy of museums, from their origins in Western Europe and
subsequent history in the United States, is clear. They are the direct offspring
of the European Enlightenment and Western rationalism, defined by the binary
division of "culture" on the one hand and "nature" on the other, with the collateral creation of disciplinary subdivisions that have been with us for centuries.

Apart from the wellsprings of its substantive beginnings, the definition
seems quite "internal" and "internalized." Yes, reference is made to being in
the "service of society," and hopefully it "communicates and exhibits" to the
public for its "education, study and enjoyment." But even within the words of
the definition, let alone a century and a half of museum practice, the operating
assumption undergirding the "knowledge" and "content" to be addressed is
that it occurs inside the museum and is to be communicated unilaterally to the

public—the originating and long-standing vision of the museum as the "temple on the hill."

Let me cite a contrasting vision. The words, stated in 1990, belong to the then secretary of the Smithsonian, Robert McCormick Adams, about the National Museum of the American Indian (NMAI):

> This is [a] . . . national museum that takes . . . the authenticity . . . the vitality . . . and the self-determination of the Native American voices . . . as the fundamental reality . . . it must represent. . . .
>
> [W]e move decisively from the older image of a museum as a temple with its superior, self-governing priesthood . . . to a forum . . . committed not to the promulgation of received wisdom but to the encouragement of a multicultural dialogue.

His words were museum-specific. But Adams's comments and their relevance went far beyond the NMAI, and my observations here do, too. Indeed, they reflect the motivating factors and results of the vast changes in museology and museum practice as the twentieth century has become the twenty-first.

WHAT ARE THESE CHANGES?

Turning first to the "what," a pivot to the historical and societal context is helpful. What happened in the museum community was linked to and then, in turn, reflected the "multiculturalism movement" in the United States that occurred during the late 1980s and 1990s. In that era, marginalized cultural communities, frequently minorities and people of color, challenged—often successfully—their continued marginalization. They strove to become recognized and respected threads in the fabric of America's cultural tapestry. The movement evolved in various forms and affected an array of existing institutions, social, political, and economic.

In the museum community, it manifested itself in the promotion of the "ethnic-specific museum" as an alternative to the reluctance, historically, of many mainstream and encyclopedic museums to address the misrepresentation of marginalized communities with consistency and diligence. At inception, the NMAI was an example of this museum typology. The first prong of its maiden mission statement was the invocation in interpretation and representation of first-person Native voice as expert and authoritative—in addition to other sources of third-party curation, which had been the historical norm and practice.

The entire 2004 opening suite of core installations at the NMAI's principal public facility on the National Mall in Washington, D.C.—*Our Universes*, *Our Peoples*, and *Our Lives*—was driven by this interpretive approach and methodology. At the time it was recognized as highly innovative museology, and in the same breath often subjected to withering critiques as the anti-intellectual product of unlettered curators who sat beyond the walls of the temple.

Over time, this interpretive deconstruction of old paradigms and the re-construction of new ones vaulted the walls of ethnic-specific institutions and began permeating encyclopedic museums of all typologies. The Autry Museum of the American West's 2017 exhibition *La Raza* is an exemplar. It addressed one of the most tumultuous periods in the civil rights history of the Chicano/Chicana community in Los Angeles, the years 1967–1977, through the lens of the photographers employed by the legendary publication of the same name. The show was cocurated by the Autry's chief curator and Luiz Garza, who was a *La Raza* photographer and remains a prominent member of the Latinx community in Los Angeles.

The Autry lens is "intercultural" as well as "multicultural." The exhibition *Empire and Liberty* addressed, to the surprise of many visitors, America's Civil War and its considerable impact on the American West. There the cultural voices were multiple and often first-person: White, Native, Chinese American, and others. Many different stories and perspectives were presented, all of them authentic, all of them based on authoritative and multiple voices.

WHY ARE THESE CHANGES OCCURRING?

The "why" of the interpretive practice I have just described is as important, or more so, than the "what." The premise is simple yet complex: on a global basis, not all systems of knowledge descend neatly and categorically, as historically most museums in Europe and the United States do, from the Enlightenment and Western rationalism. Indeed, based on a global perspective, very few do.

New Zealand academics Penny Allan and Huhana Smith emphasize this point with respect to the Maori community in New Zealand in an article they wrote for *MAI Journal*:

> Importantly a . . . Maori approach to science is not based on the dualistic assumptions of a Western science epistemology. The distinctions or separation between professional scientist and non-scientific stakeholder, theory and practice, subject and object, start and finish, past and present are subsumed by a holistic approach that considers a whole-of-person, and a whole-of-system theory of knowing.

Thus, the inclusive engagement of curatorial "voice," especially the first-person voice, with respect to knowledge systems that fall outside the realm of Western thought is more than a gratuitous political gesture. To the contrary, if museums are to communicate knowledge most fulsomely, completely, and accurately, that inclusion is essential.

A TRANSFORMATION ONGOING

The foregoing "what" and "why" of my discussion segue into the final component of my argument regarding museum definitions—namely, the impact of what I have already addressed on the very fundamentals of museology and museum practice in the twenty-first century. In a sentence: the times have changed, and museum definitions need to adapt, not to the exclusion of all that has been, but to the inclusion of what might also be in the future. The popular, conventional, and historical public perception of museums as principally worthy cultural destinations to visit occasionally needs to be altered, in definition and practice, in the name of sound epistemological practice, social relevance, and broader public connection and impact. In short, the twenty-first-century museum can and should be far more than a stop on the tour bus route.

I return to Adams's declaration for support of this proposition. His, for its time, was a material recasting of museology, museum practice, and conventional interpretive curatorial and interpretive methodology: the demise of the temple on the hill with its self-appointed priesthood, the explicit invocation and affirmation of first-person and multiple curatorial voices and their authority, the recognition and endorsement of distinctive and differing knowledge systems and their validity.

All of the foregoing turned conventional museology and museum practice on its head, from top down to bottom up, inside out to outside in, bilateralism instead of unilateralism, dialogue instead of monologue. That wholesale transformation in approach is seminal and has a direct impact on the very nature of the museum as a community-connected, multivocal gathering space and place of broader civic and societal import "committed not to the promulgation of received wisdom but to the encouragement of a multicultural dialogue."

If the era of COVID-19 and Black Lives Matter has taught us nothing else, surely it has demonstrated that currently in the United States—and we are hardly alone—we struggle to find and implement civic and social space. We desperately need gathering places for discussion, discourse, debate, even controversy; we need forums and safe places for unsafe ideas concerning cultural history and human experience, past and present. As defined and described above, museums can serve as a notable and valuable chink in that contemporary armor of political and social polarities and the disabling cultural and historical gloom they engender.

The museum as counterpoint, although not able to do everything, can do something—and a very important something. That hope should be the social, museological, and institutional aspiration of all museums and how they define themselves and their futures in the twenty-first century. Museum definitions that fail to consider and, indeed, embrace a future of continuing societal relevance and impact put museums at risk of becoming public institutions diminished and distant in history's rearview mirror.

Part Two

Safe Places or Social Spaces?

5

The Purpose of Place

Diana Pardue

Museums are committed to being recognized as meaningful meeting places, open and diverse platforms for learning, exchange, and progress. What should be the role of museums in a time of social scrutiny and transformation? What actions can be taken to provide a wide and inclusive experience to share knowledge and promote understanding in a safe environment for all? Are museums addressing the conflicts and challenges of the present? Do they safeguard and present diverse memories and guarantee equal access to heritage?

The discussion of these concepts points to a global need for museums to rethink their missions and develop new strategies to create safe and trusted social spaces.

Three distinguished essayists, Linda Norris, Ihor Poshyvailo, and Andrés Roldán, provide an enlightened, insightful discussion of this topic in this section. The goal of this discussion was to determine ways in which museums can be transformed from being considered merely "social spaces" where people gather into "safe places" where people not only feel represented but also at full liberty to have difficult conversations about subjects that might not easily be addressed in other environments.

In Linda Norris's words, these two concepts, social or safe spaces, are not necessarily in conflict, and it is when museums embrace both aspects that they obtain their full potential as spaces where a feeling of safety and belonging will help achieve the best of any social experience. We would like to think that it is the job of museums not only to preserve unique collections but also to ensure that the human stories linked to these collections are not forgotten and are interpreted in a just and inclusive manner. Norris's essay takes on the concept of "yes, and" in the discussion of museum spaces being identified as both social and safe. She describes how institutions can work to meet both criteria, creating safe spaces not only for their objects but also for people—their visitors and, particularly, their staff members. The social aspect can be achieved through intentional, designed, and facilitated dialogue with visitors to the museum and with members of the museum's surrounding community. The desired end result is for museums to do the job of authentically telling human stories, in all forms, so that our experiences can be shared, remembered, and honored now and into the future.

Meanwhile, both Poshyvailo and Roldán talk from personal experience. Poshyvailo shares the importance of democratization of cultural spaces in Ukraine after the renewal of its statehood; Roldán explains the significant influence a community-centered science museum had in the transformation of Medellín as part of the strategy to invigorate a city that had been severely affected by the drug war and social disruption in Colombia. Poshyvailo's experience around the difficulties faced during the democratization of government-controlled cultural spaces in Ukraine constitutes a great example of how social spaces, dedicated to the dissemination of Soviet indoctrination, were transformed into safe spaces, shifting "from autocratic propaganda machines into open democratic platforms serving society, encouraging dialogue and reconciliation, rethinking conflicted and traumatic past, rediscovering identity, and promoting understanding, peace and social justice."

Roldán's experience makes us aware of the impact that the creation of a socially committed museum can have in rewriting the narrative on what used to be considered one of the most dangerous cities in the world: "Our challenge was to transform science into a social component that could bring about new ways of communication between communities, a new way to understand our own problems, our identity, our origins, and a way to interconnect other kinds of values in a society that had long suffered from intense social conflict."

Four themes emerged from this very informative and instructive discussion drawn from these three notable writers. First, museums should use their collections as testimony, along with their story, to create change in a more just way, particularly with their communities; Rick West's concept of collections as means to an end and not ends in themselves emerges again in these particular examples and gains strength as a way in which space can acquire that desired "safe" qualification.

The second point is that museums should focus on creating narratives for their community rather than creating narratives for other museum curators. And that is the importance of working with external versus internal audiences and bilateralism versus unilateralism. There, again, is the continuation of the theme of how museums move and whom they are actually serving. Norris's essay addresses an important matter that has reached even more significance during the pandemic era: the fact that museums should begin by guaranteeing the safety of their own staff as an example and starting point of their desired social responsibility.

The third idea is that museums should represent multiple points of view, voices of authority and authenticity. They should encompass and communicate the affective and engage and intersect communities reflecting the human stories to be remembered. It begins within the museum and expands to other places. It gives new meaning to what museums do with the collections that sit in their buildings and make them unique. In Roldán's words, "the museum becomes a tool in which what happens inside is not only defined by its collections, by its phenomena, or by the immersive situations it can create. In this scenario, collections and phenomena are meant to have a social role. This helps us understand the place we live in, its history, its collective memory, and the ways in which the world works, as a means to help us improve as a society."

Finally, the fourth point is that museums are places and spaces of social transformation, bringing people together in a common understanding, but at the same time challenging existing narratives that can be uncomfortable, even dangerous for some people. As Poshyvailo states in his essay, "today museums help us to reconstruct the past, reflect on the fundamental social values, and provide a background essential for the reconciliation of society and understanding of the present. Such institutions can be highly trusted, multicultural forums for discussing controversial issues, gaining mutual understanding, and even consolidating and healing communities from post-conflict and post-disaster traumas."

And so, it all begins with what is currently known about museums, but it transcends its walls into wider spaces and more inclusive goals, transforming our temple idea of a museum into a forum where many different voices can gather and hopefully become instrumental in societal reconciliation and mutual understanding.

6

Museums and Place

Alejandra Peña Gutíerrez with Andrés Roldán

Andrés Roldán is the general director of Parque Explora, Colombia's largest science museum, aquarium, and planetarium. Roldán works with his team on the creation of compelling and innovative learning environments to promote cultural engagement. He also aims to open the museum's walls, taking it to different territories and communities, educational strategies, community processes, and itinerant experiences to connect people through learning experiences. As an active participant in Medellín's transformation, Roldán's work is based on the model of a socially committed museum. He believes the union between education, culture, urban planning, and architecture is vital for fostering sustainable community development and social justice.

Alejandra Peña Gutíerrez: According to your own experience, could you describe the impact Parque Explora has had on the transformation of Medellín and the development of its community?

Andrés Roldán: I want to start with a piece of personal history. I am an industrial designer. I graduated in the late 1990s and was invited to participate in a conversation about the creation of a new science center for Medellín.

In the early 2000s, Medellín was considered the most dangerous city in the world, with a rising number of deaths due to Colombia's drug war and internal conflicts. In such a challenging environment, the idea of developing a museum was, in fact, part of a vision of how to reframe the narrative of the city itself.

Parque Explora and other cultural institutions were set up along the city to bring a sense of dignity to the communities that had become more vulnerable in these adverse circumstances.

Libraries, museums, and the public transportation systems became interconnected and intertwined to create new educational environments.

Building this new museum was the equivalent of being given a blank canvas where each stroke would help depict the final picture for the future of our community.

Peña: You have been an advocate for bringing awareness to how education, design, and urban planning combined can contribute to social transformation. Could you tell us how this concept came to life with the development of Parque Explora?

Roldán: The site for this science center was located beside the old city dump, which was later transformed into an informally populated neighborhood.

The origin of our science museum was very different from the traditional science or natural history museum, where machinery, artifacts, and tools are normally displayed to promote innovation, as well as to preserve collections for further scientific studies. In an environment such as Medellín, the creation of a science center brought a different sense to the meaning of science, as well as to what this might represent to its community. Our concept was centered not only on the display of achievements or innovations of the scientific or technological world, but our goal also became to display those tools of reality that could help us understand the ways in which we can connect with the world and within ourselves.

The distinctive feature of our museology was based on the premise of approaching science not as a goal, but as a tool for social transformation. Our challenge was to transform science into a social component that could bring about new ways of communication between communities, a new way to understand our own problems, our identity, our origins, and a way to interconnect other kinds of values in a society that had long suffered from intense social conflict.

Peña: Could you talk about how the museum has found ways to "dilute" its walls in your search to benefit the local communities?

Roldán: The role of Parque Explora was, from the beginning, conceived as functional, with a mission to inspire, communicate with, and transform our audiences through memorable learning adventures in interactive scenarios that could contribute to the appropriation of knowledge. Such memorable experiences are conceived as events or lived processes, which, through impactful content, innovative formats, and inclusive conversations can stimulate our visitors and contribute to a better understanding of the world.

The museum becomes a tool in which what happens inside is not defined only by its collections, by its phenomena, or by the immersive situations it can create. In this scenario, collections and phenomena are meant to have a social role. This helps us understand the place we live in, its history, its collective memory, and the ways in which the world works, as a means to help us improve as a society.

This social architecture is meant to develop healthier communities, which will then interconnect with healthier societies. This museum is conceived not just as a tool for inspiration, but as an agora for conversation and creation—a lab where people can create, a tool that will influence the interaction with other territories and neighborhoods, to foster new conversations among people from different environments. The definition of our museum is not limited by what we have, but by what we can achieve.

Our mission has been defined by our ability to develop learning experiences as a means for social transformation. Ultimately, our concept would not even require a building or a particular object; however, you need the skills and methodologies to create new content that will help interconnect the communities in a more empathetic, more creative, more curious, and therefore a much healthier way.

Parque Explora has a contemporary perspective of what museums should be. We have become a community where thinking collides; we enable intersections and interactions between communities that would not necessarily interact under different circumstances.

Any new definition of a museum should consider at least two basic concepts: first, the acknowledgment of our social role and our ability to provide our communities with a better grasp of every component of our existence, from history to science and art; and, second, the reaffirmation that we are important tools when it comes to showcasing the capabilities, the achievements, and the creativity of our own audiences. Museums should become not only displayers or speakers, but also receptors and promoters of everyone's talents and capabilities.

Peña: Science is a very defined thing, and it's not particularly inclusive in terms of its history; your concept of a science center has probably encountered controversy or potential resistance. Please share not only what you have done when encountering some points of resistance, but also what you're trying to do in creating a science museum where that resistance comes from.

Roldán: Not being under the umbrella of a research or scientific institution provided a lot of liberty when we set up our science center. I believe objects themselves should not define the mission of the museum; objects are an excuse for social interaction—it is the museum's responsibility to create experiences around these objects to help develop our interpretation of the world.

Many museums are preceded by a long history of collecting. The origin of museums comes from the overgrowth of cabinets of curiosities.

Many other museums were defined by the spirit of their own buildings. But the museums of the twenty-first century should be defined not by their objects or their buildings but by the interaction with their communities. This is the basic concept that should be pushing the new definition of "museum."

The way in which we frame the situations that we create within our exhibitions, and the phenomena built around the objects, are the real tools that will allow us to encourage conversations and situations that will help with our understanding of the world.

Even natural history museums must aspire to accomplish a more comprehensive understanding of the present and future of our everyday lives, adding to their discourse the contributions that result from interactions with visitors.

On a universal perspective, this new museum definition will consider important topics such as heritage, collections, and the preservation of a collective memory, but at the end of the day, what matters most is the interaction with our audiences, the impact on our communities, and the effect all of this has on the neighborhoods that surround us.

Alejandra Peña Gutíerrez with Andrés Roldán

7

Yes, and

MUSEUMS AS SAFE *AND* SOCIAL SPACES

Linda Norris

If you've ever watched an improvisational comedy troupe, you might have seen folks engaging in the concept of "yes, and." It's built on the idea of one participant accepting what another participant brought to the table ("yes"), and then expanding on that line of thinking ("and"). The idea of museums as safe *or* social spaces is often presented as a dichotomy. This brings to mind a variation of these two options: a cozy, warm space *or* a space filled with partygoers. But when we expand those concepts and design ways for spaces to be both safe *and* social, museums can reach their full potential. Museums can and should be social places for safety and safe spaces to have social experiences.

I write from the International Coalition of Sites of Conscience (ICSC), an International Council of Museums–affiliated organization. ICSC is a network of more than three hundred members in sixty-seven countries around the globe—museums, historic sites, parks, and memory initiatives—that use the power of history to create a more just present. Sites of Conscience share a common set of values no matter where each site is located, no matter the subject matter addressed, no matter the size of its budget and staff, no matter its number of visitors. These are the values of the power of memory, the inclusion of many voices, and the commitment to using the past to inform the present and create a better future.

Sites of Conscience members include historic places that one might expect—Maison des Esclaves in Senegal, the Kigali Genocide Memorial in Rwanda, and the Tuol Sleng Genocide Museum in Cambodia. But Sites of Conscience members are also museums and historic sites that have expanded the way they consider their work beyond traditional museum practice, including the

Statue of Liberty/Ellis Island and the Missouri History Museum in the United States, the Tea Plantation Workers Museum and Archive in Sri Lanka, Our Lord in the Attic historic house museum in the Netherlands, and the Memorial of Small Farmers Leagues and Struggles in rural Brazil. Sites of Conscience, including those highlighted in this essay, provide concrete models for a new definition of "museum"—institutions that are inclusive, accessible, and engaged with their communities.

SAFE SPACES: SAFE FOR OBJECTS ONLY?

Historically, museums have prioritized the safety of their objects above all else. To be clear, that "safety" was primarily extended to objects made, related to, or controlled (and often stolen) by the White majorities of the United States and European nations. In the United States and Canada, a small but increasing number of museums have entered into agreements with Indigenous populations so that sacred objects may be loaned and reused for traditional spiritual and cultural practices. However, the guidelines for loans to non-museum entities set forth by the American Alliance of Museums (AAM) state, after a cautionary opening paragraph:

> If a museum engages in the practice of loaning objects from the collection to organizations other than museums, such a practice should be considered for its appropriateness to the museum's mission; be thoughtfully managed with the utmost care and in compliance with the most prudent practices in collections stewardship, ensuring that loaned objects receive the level of care, documentation and control at least equal to that given to the objects that remain on the premises; and be governed by clearly defined and approved institutional policies and procedures, including a collections management policy and code of ethics.[1]

In this context, "safe" means a set of museum standards, with scant attention paid to the safety of source communities where the objects have deep meaning and significance.

SAFE SPACES—FOR MUSEUM WORKERS?

As a field, we need to begin creating museums that are safe spaces for everyone who works in them. Museum leadership needs to support fair pay, address issues of harassment, serve as key allies, work to diversify staffs and boards of directors, and provide much more than lip service to the physical and emotional needs of museum workers. During the pandemic, in the United States, many museums laid off staff—particularly public-facing and education department staff, while endowments continued to rise in value and those in leadership maintained their jobs and salaries. A 2021 survey by AAM found that 43 percent of people in the museum sector have lost income as a result of the COVID-19 pandemic, with the average decline in earnings amounting to

Linda Norris

31 percent. The United Kingdom Museums Association estimates that 4,690 museum workers had lost their positions as of October 2021. The growing number of museum unionization efforts is a testament to the vital need for a social safety net for workers. Individually led, crowd-sourced efforts in both the United States and the United Kingdom provided short-term emergency funding for museum workers under economic stress (e.g., Paula Santos and others raised more than $100,000 in the Museum Workers Relief Fund, which supported U.S. workers).[2]

The lack of safety for staff isn't just a lack of financial security. In every area of museum operations, staff are being asked to take on additional responsibilities that may involve activities that touch on generations-long trauma or responsibilities that result in difficult conversations with visitors on everything from mask wearing to the legacy of enslaved people in the United States. Museum leaders need to understand trauma and develop ways to support staff in working through both individual and collective trauma. These efforts cannot be one-off workshops but need to be designed and supported throughout all museum operations, with a clear understanding from leadership about the critical nature of this support.

Museum thinker Rainey Tisdale shared these strategies for organizations addressing community trauma in a Sites of Conscience workshop, which I have adapted slightly, as approaches for addressing the trauma within museum organizations:

- Attend to your own trauma first—you can't help your community if your bucket is overflowing.
- Train your staff in trauma-informed practice and emotional first aid.
- Build relationships and collaborations with your community's mental-health workers.
- Acknowledge the trauma your museum staff is experiencing; destigmatize it and give it language.
- Develop your site's capacity to serve as a holding space for staff members. Where can they reflect, relax, and find support in the work space?
- Offer opportunities to practice resilience strategies and/or to metabolize trauma through movement. Can a staff meeting begin with a moment of reflection or by sharing moments of joy? What about organizing walking meetings?
- Attend to the anniversaries of traumatic events. Even a large event such as the global pandemic has individual iterations for each of us: the last time we were in the office, the day colleagues were laid off, and more. Make time to acknowledge the sense of hurt in these.[3]

Think of staff as an asset that is as important—and deserving of the same thoughtful, dedicated care—as the objects in your museum collections.

SAFE *AND* SOCIAL SPACES COMBINED

The word "social" has a bit of a cocktail party connotation. The idea that museums are social spaces implies to some people that museums are party places, rather than centers for learning and contemplation. Walk into any museum, however, and it's abundantly clear that most museum visits are social. It's the rare museum visitor who comes on her own. Most visitors come with families, with friends, as a part of a tour group, or even, as Barack and Michelle Obama did, together on a first date. Social connections are a way to process new information, to share ideas, and to reflect on past histories.

Facilitated dialogue—in group gatherings, in exhibitions, or on tours—is always a social experience, but it is one that provides museum and historic site visitors and community members with opportunities to connect, learn, and understand perspectives different from their own. It is geared toward the express goals of personal and collective learning. Bringing together people in social situations to learn more must be intentional. Museum workers cannot only hope that conversation happens—we must design it. At the Harriet Beecher Stowe Center in Hartford, Connecticut, intensive prototyping now provides visitors with an opportunity, on a guided tour, to sit together to peruse writings, cartoons, and songs from the 1850s and then engage in deep conversation with strangers about the complex legacies of slavery in America today. At the Matilda Joslyn Gage House in upstate New York, bright yellow footprints on a floor encourage visitors to face each other to engage in conversations. In Philadelphia, Eastern State Penitentiary's award-winning exhibition begins with the question, "Have you ever broken the law?" "Yes" answers take one path to start the exhibit; "no" answers take another. Each path provides provocative questions that encourage visitors to consider the history and present-day realities of mass incarceration in the United States.

At the Museum of Free Derry, a project of the Bloody Sunday Trust in Northern Ireland, the social space is an activist space where the continued quest for justice for victims of Bloody Sunday is an ongoing social process. The museum describes its work: "The Museum of Free Derry tells the story of how a largely working-class community rose up against the years of oppression it had endured. The museum and archive have become an integral part of Ireland's radical and civil rights heritage."

The museum also tells the story of Bloody Sunday, the day when the British Army committed mass murder on the streets of the Bogside. It tells the story of how the people of Derry, led by the families of the victims, overcame the injustice and wrote a new chapter in the history of civil rights, which has become a source of international inspiration. The museum is a public space where the concept of Free Derry can be explored in both historic and contemporary contexts. The struggle of Free Derry is part of a wider struggle in Ireland and internationally for freedom and equality for all.

This work of the Museum of Free Derry—the work of accountability, justice, and reconciliation—is collective work, through marches, meetings, exhibits, collecting, and, most recently, the museum's effort to share its Conflict Transformation Model with other communities emerging from conflict. This project brings together individuals from all sides in Northern Ireland: Loyalist and Republican combatants, flute bands, Orange boys, and individuals from both the British Army and the Royal Ulster Constabulary. In Northern Ireland, as in so many other communities, the traumas and need for healing are generational.[4]

The process of creating safe spaces for generations of those whose stories have been purposely omitted from mainstream narratives is complex and often lengthy. The Montpelier Descendants Committee comprises descendants of the more than three hundred African Americans enslaved at the home of James Madison, the fourth president of the United States. In June 2021, the Montpelier Foundation's board of directors voted to approve by-laws that establish equality with the Descendants Committee. "This historic decision means that for the first time, the descendants of enslaved persons at a major national historic site will be co-equals in sharing governing power and responsibility for the very site that enslaved their ancestors," said Gene Hickok, chair of the board of directors. A safe space means that voices are heard, and power is shared.[5]

But it's important not to dismiss the value of a good party! Constitution Hill in South Africa, a Site of Conscience, has hosted the Afro-Punk Festival. Some people wondered why an Afro-Punk Festival was being held at a former prison and present-day constitutional court. The museum responded, saying that "for us in terms of what we stand for, constitutionalism, democracy, human rights, this festival is ideal. It completely aligns with what we stand for as custodians of South Africa's constitutional history."[6]

SAFE FOR EVERYONE?

It's a mistake to believe that every perspective deserves a safe space in a museum. Museums are not and have never been neutral, despite what many museumgoers think and what some museum directors may still believe. The art on the walls, the label text, the composition of a governing board and staff—each of those elements has values embedded within them, either implicitly or explicitly. Work is just beginning to be done now to balance those "neutral" but not *actually* unbiased presentations. Equally important, we need to be clear that the voices of intolerance are not welcome in museum settings. As one example, the Canadian Museum for Human Rights in Winnipeg has a code of conduct that is explicit in addressing this issue:

> We welcome the exchange of ideas through respectful discussion that advances understanding about human rights. Anyone whose conduct is abusive, disruptive or disrespectful . . . may be asked to leave our building. We also reserve the right to remove social media posts that violate this code of

conduct—and to permanently block serious or repeat offenders. While diverse perspectives are welcome, the Museum is committed to the fundamental principle that all human beings are born equal in dignity and rights.[7]

Over the past two years, everyone has become familiar with online museum activities. This new platform presents new challenges in making spaces safe for ideas and dialogue. Old Salem Museum and Gardens in Winston-Salem, North Carolina, has a robust TikTok presence. It began with videos about crafts and other museum activities, but in 2021, staff members began making TikToks that explore the legacy of enslaved Africans at the site. Almost a million views later, it has become clear that a space to discuss these issues among TikTok users was greatly needed. The museum itself made clear, in respectful but firm online responses, that it was not a safe space for racism and hatred. The staff was dedicated to supporting one another, and the result was a greatly expanded civic space.[8]

People bring their emotions to museum experiences, along with their intellectual and physical selves. Research has shown that we learn more and remember better when emotions are engaged. Visitors may need space alone or space together to process those emotions. Our museums can be those spaces, both solitary and social, by creating opportunities for both individual and collective reflection for larger societal impact. The War Childhood Museum (WCM) in Sarajevo, Bosnia and Herzegovina, recently developed the exhibition *Speaking Out*, aimed to give voice to conflict-related sexual violence (CRSV) survivors and to raise awareness of CRSV in Bosnian and Herzegovinian society, which is often ignored more than twenty-five years after the war. The exhibition featured body maps, a technique in which one tells a story through a life-size drawing of his body. Said Amina Kravavec, director of WCM:

> The body-mapping workshop provided the Conflict-Related Sexual Violence (CRSV) survivors with alternative means of communication about the difficult past experiences, but it also, perhaps even more importantly, enabled deeper reflection—through this introspective process, the workshop participants became more aware of their emotions and strengths, all the while gaining access to the internal resources that have been buried deep inside. By contributing to individual healing processes, this workshop also paved way for the healing processes taking place on a collective level.[9]

SAFE AND SOCIAL FOR THE FUTURE

A few years ago, I visited the Cambodian National Museum in Phnom Penh. During the Khmer Rouge's control of the country in the 1970s, the museum was closed and abandoned. Many museum staff were killed during that time, and artifacts were stolen or damaged. The museum has reopened, and today staff are working to care for and share an incredible collection of art. On a hot day, I wandered through the galleries and then out to a cool, shaded porch. Off to

Linda Norris

one side, a teacher was instructing two young people in traditional Cambodian dance.

Traditional dance, like so many traditions in Cambodia, was decimated by the Khmer Rouge. Teachers and master dancers were killed, and the art form was almost lost. I sat watching dancers do the same graceful movements that I saw depicted on the ancient statues inside the museum. This was a space that was both social and safe. As a watcher, I felt connected and, more important, those dancers felt safe and social in learning and sharing a vital tradition. That's our job as museums: to ensure that human stories, whatever form they come in—as art, as artifact, as place—are not forgotten, and that the remembering and sharing can bring us together to create more just futures for everyone.

NOTES

1. "Loaning Collections to Non-Museum Entities," American Alliance of Museums, https://www.aam-us.org/programs/ethics-standards-and-professional-practices/loaning-collections-to-non-museum-entities/.
2. "Measuring the Impact of Covid 19 on People in the Museum Field," American Alliance of Museums, https://www.aam-us.org/wp-content/uploads/2021/04/Measuring-the-Impact-of-COVID-19-on-People-in-the-Museum-Field-Report.pdf; "Redundancy Tracker," Museums Association, https://www.museumsassociation.org/campaigns/workforce/redundancy-tracker/; "Museum Workers Relief Fund," GoFundMe, https://www.gofundme.com/f/museum-workers-speak-relief-fund.
3. Adapted from Rainey Tisdale, webinar for International Coalition of Sites of Conscience, 2021.
4. See the Museum of Free Derry website, https://museumoffreederry.org/.
5. "James Madison's Montpelier Votes to Share Power with Descendants of Plantations Enslaved People," National Trust for Historic Preservation, June 18, 2021, https://savingplaces.org/press-center/media-resources/montpelier-votes-to-share-power-with-descendants-of-plantations-enslaved-people#.YWwzQBBKjDI.
6. "Afro-Punk," Constitution Hill, https://www.constitutionhill.org.za/signature-events/2017/afropunk-joburg.
7. "Code of Conduct," Canadian Museum for Human Rights, https://humanrights.ca/code-of-conduct.
8. "Webinar Shorts: TikTok, Trolls and Sites of Conscience," webinar, International Coalition of Sites of Conscience, https://zoom.us/rec/play/1_-vIrFbrKgPDXXhQBcsc EYHKGXTA3kGnW5Ny-euWZxSWgeI0wey2inz4-V7aNRLCIrK0IeMzi3zK bxD.mHh6s0Whep9HQ0jZ?continueMode=true&_x_zm_rtaid=HBceBC 3gQm-UjuQqQiAdyQ.1634563487063.0e9eaa6d33192e768850d9028e4f 1cad&_x_zm_rhtaid=635.
9. Amina Kravavec, interview with Ashley Nelson, International Coalition of Sites of Conscience, October 2021.

8

Crossing Museum Boundaries

FROM GALLERY SPACE TO PROTEST PLACE

Ihor Poshyvailo

This essay stems from my contribution to the webinar "What Is a Museum?" presented by the United States Committee of the International Council of Museums (ICOM) webinar series, which encouraged the rethinking of a museum's mission, functions, and future in a broad sense. One session was focused on the role of the museum in a time of social scrutiny and transformation, political turbulence, and global challenges. This topic was inspired, I believe, by the intensive discussions among international museum community members on a new definition of the word "museum" that occurred in 2019 at the ICOM conference in Kyoto, which I had the great privilege to attend.

Thousands of museum professionals globally challenge themselves and their institutions to reinvent their missions and identities. Are they really democratic, inclusive, and polyphonic spaces for critical dialogue about the past and the future? Are they addressing the conflicts and challenges of the present? Do they safeguard and present diverse memories and guarantee equal access to heritage? Are they safe and social places? It seems that the answer is quite simple—they are such in some countries, and they are not in many others.

Let me start by mentioning that museums today have become not only classical institutions of preservation and presentation of the past and various heritages but also important communication facilities, community engagement centers, and guardians of a nation's memory and identity. These institutions have the power to profoundly alter our knowledge and sense of ourselves and of the world around us by transmitting information and implicitly communicating "messages about authority, power, and the values of the dominant culture."[1] As Australian museologist Caroline Turner has argued, "museums in our contemporary globalized world are far more than repositories of the history of 'nations' or single national narratives. They reflect culture in its broadest sense and diverse community concerns as well as transnational ideas."[2]

No doubt, today museums help us to reconstruct the past, reflect on the fundamental social values, and provide a background essential for the reconciliation of society and understanding of the present. Such institutions can be highly trusted multicultural forums for discussing controversial issues, gaining mutual understanding, and even consolidating and healing communities' post-conflict and post-disaster traumas. But "it is important that museums are transforming into places of reconciliation—with the past and between conflict parties, but without attempts to harmonize the history," as Hans-Martin Hinz, former president of ICOM, stated at his lecture in Kyiv.[3]

This statement is of a special significance in Ukraine, where the genocide policy of the communists and cultural oppressions in the twentieth century resulted in a considerable loss of historical and cultural memories. During the repressive years of the Soviet regime, much of the distinctly Ukrainian heritage lay dormant. Throughout that period, museums were explicitly places of propaganda. They depended ideologically, economically, and administratively on the government. Since state independence in 1991, Ukrainian museums have made significant strides in making themselves more open and welcoming places, with enlarged, presented, and inclusively interpreted collections, changing exhibitions, various programs, engaged audiences, and much stronger leadership.

I started my museum career just after Ukraine renewed its statehood. Since then, I have worked for three museums located in a small village and in Ukraine's capital. Those museums were newly founded and had just started their development from scratch, but they have become highly recognized and respected institutions. I had the privilege to learn a lot about how to make museums transform and matter, being a Fulbright Scholar at the Smithsonian Institution, an international fellow at the DeVos Institute of Art Management at the Kennedy Center, as well as participating in and organizing international and local conferences, workshops, and discussions. Thus, I'm aware of how challenging it was and still is for most post-Soviet state-run museums in Ukraine to shift from autocratic propaganda machines into open, democratic platforms serving society, encouraging dialogue and reconciliation, rethinking a conflicted and traumatic past, rediscovering identity, and promoting understanding, peace, and social justice.

The Ivan Honchar Museum (Ukrainian Centre of Folk Culture) opened in Kyiv after the death of its founder, artist and collector Ivan Honchar, in 1993. Since the 1950s, his unofficial and private museum in Kyiv, which was under KGB Secret Service surveillance, has become extremely popular among young, educated, creative, and active people, who unveiled Ukrainian history and culture, and revealed their personal, cultural, and national identities due to Honchar's museum's special environment that was open to the public.

Was it a safe place for artifacts neglected and threatened by the Soviet communists and rescued by Ivan Honchar in his research field trips and cultural activities? I'm not sure, as in that period, his home museum was also an unsafe space for visitors who were taken to the KGB after their visits and meetings with the artist. Many times, his artworks (historical sculptures) were ruined under pressure from the authorities. But, at the same time, it was a unique social space that served people and provided access to their neglected, forbidden, and imprisoned heritage. I had the privilege of being familiar with Honchar and to work at the state-run museum based on his private collection for almost two decades. That was a fantastic time to rethink the general museum concept of "serving people" in the face of brutal realities.

Much later, in the context of the Euromaidan revolutionary events in Ukraine of 2013–2014, the combination of the simple words "museum with people" has gained a new and specific meaning to me. My reflections were activated by my American colleague and friend Linda Norris, who on December 1, 2013, published the post "If I Ran a Museum in Kyiv, Right Now" on her blog, *The Uncatalogued Museum*.[4] It was a prompt trans-Atlantic and transcultural response of the museum expert, well known in Ukraine due to her activities as a Fulbright Scholar, to the night attack of riot police on the peaceful protesters, mostly students. A wave of demonstrations and civil unrest began in late November 2013, caused by a massive public outpouring for closer integration with Europe. Guy Verhofstadt, member of the European Parliament, former prime minister of Belgium, claimed that it was the biggest pro-European demonstration in the history of the European Union. Victoria Nuland, U.S. assistant secretary of state for European and Eurasian affairs, underscored in December 2013 that Euromaidan was a symbol of the power of civil society: "This movement is about justice, civil rights and the people's demands to have a government that listens to them, that represents their interests and that respects them."[5]

In her blog post, Norris puts herself in the shoes of a Ukrainian museum director and offers an action program in three spheres: representing community values and ethics, serving the community, and collecting. In particular, she would make a public statement first and then take a look at the ethical practices and transparency of her own museum, throw open its doors, and invite the public in for free. Keeping the museum open early and late, she would have cups of hot tea ready, provide a warm place for reflection and contemplation, and find a space in the gallery for people to write or draw about their hopes and fears, encouraging participants to think about Ukraine as a nation, about beauty, truth, and complicated histories. Even more—she would permit and even encourage the staff to take part in the protests, if they so desired, in protecting their values and future. If Linda were the director of the history museum, she would be out collecting lots of potential exhibits for the future, starting with tweets and Facebook postings, oral histories, flags, banners, and handmade signs and photographs to metal barriers, face-masked helmets, and police uniforms, even homemade antidotes to tear gas.

Indeed, this is a natural and seemingly common response for a community leader or leadership of an American museum—a museum that is "about," "for," and "with" people. That was the topic for discussion that my Portuguese colleague Maria Vlachou proposed at the European Museum Advisors Conference in Lisbon a few years ago. In particular, she investigated whether John Cotton Dana's "tomorrow museum" is already here, one hundred years later, and analyzed inclusion and involvement developments in the relationship between museums and society: "They started telling stories (they were 'about' people), they told stories using a language most people would understand (they were 'for' people) and nowadays they invite people to help choose the stories that are going to be told (they are 'with' people)."[6] It seems quite important for cultural institutions to share authority with the community and improve the ways in which they are present and connected to their communities—for example, during the Boston Marathon bombing or after Hurricane Sandy, when these organizations should be able "to communicate rapidly and effectively . . . be nimble, flexible and responsive . . . to societal events."[7]

In that dramatic winter of Euromaidan protest, I kept asking myself and my colleagues, especially in the periods of social unrest and political tensions: Do our museums, their leadership, and staff really want and know how to be with people and protect their dignity, cultural property, and spaces? How they can be responsive and inclusive to the needs of society and communities they represent and serve? These were the questions asked of my colleagues and me in the publication "Museums of Ukraine and Euromaidan: Learning to Be with the People," released in mid-December 2013.

The voice of the museum community in Ukraine in that period was not that loud, but it was quite distinct. A dozen or so museums made public statements against the government's repressive actions against freedom, dignity, and human rights, and opened their doors to protesters, giving them tea, rest, and cultural programming. And, of course, a lot of museum teams started to act.

For example, the Ivan Honchar Museum in that period took its educational and cultural programs out of its building to a protest space in Independence Square, named Maidan. I was among a group of museum professionals who documented the events and supported the people. Soon we had envisioned the creation of a new institution, Museum of Maidan (Museum of Freedom), which could become a platform for dialogue and critical thinking, a safe place for unsafe ideas, and a model for transition and change for post-Soviet Ukrainian museums. Various institutions and individuals worldwide, including the U.S. Embassy, the Smithsonian Institution, ICOM, International Coalition of Sites of Consciousness, International Centre for the Study of the Preservation and Restoration of Cultural Property, Fulbright Ukraine, and my American friends and colleagues, including Norris, Elaine Heumann Gurian, James Volkert, and many others, professionally supported our grassroots initiative.

Now we are in a process of actively developing a new state-run institution, the National Memorial to the Heavenly Hundred and Revolution of Dignity Museum (Maidan Museum), which strives to correspond to the new ICOM definition of "museum" but, at the same time, faces again and again the unfolding challenges due to the social and political turbulence in Ukraine in this postcolonial period of democratization, reforms, and protecting its independence in the ongoing Russian-Ukrainian war.

In this connection we should admit that creating such museums as open platforms and spaces for diverse memories and dialogue is not always welcomed by authorities who still strive to control the dominant ideology and political influences, as well as the museum's role in strengthening civil society and democratization of the nation. So, how should museums behave in the deep conflict between authorities and society? Should they be neutral, or at least pretend to be neutral?, as David Fleming, a director of National Museums Liverpool, discussed at his keynote speech at the 2014 American Alliance of Museums meeting in Seattle, exploring the roles of modern museums, how political they are, and whether this poses a threat or opportunity.[8]

Different museums used to develop their own approaches to the representation of acute topics for the public. As Fiona Cameron, a culture and museum expert from Australia, suggested in her article "Safe Places for Unsafe Ideas? History and Science Museums, Hot Topics and Moral Predicaments," museum visitors, on the one hand, seek open discussion and a pluralistic presentation in museums; on the other hand, they request that museums establish moral norms and orientations to understand and evaluate social behavior.[9]

By developing exhibitions and programs for presenting and interpreting a complicated history, catastrophes, or "bad news," museums should ensure that their visitors have the opportunity to learn the history nonlinearly, with a mandatory visionary message for the future, outlining landmarks and values of social progress, immersion in a broad context, and not just getting formal, factual materials about the past and the present. However, as British researcher Andrew Whitmarsh stated, museum curators often try to put off for later the discussion of complicated things or controversial topics. Such historical museums follow the path of political concepts as institutions of memory not by producing new meanings but only by strengthening the existing ones, promoting discussions and debates, and acting more as moderators, bridges between different parties.[10]

Gurian, a world-renowned museum consultant, engaged in crafting the Maidan Museum, advises that the concept of a "bad news" institution should include a process of multilevel consultations, cooperation with representatives of various parties to the conflict, and being healing and inclusive. It is important that such museums serve as platforms of dialogue where opposite opinions should not necessarily be fully accepted but at least discussed. For this, Gurian considers that two types of people are needed—"authentic witnesses" (charismatic leaders of a protest movement) and "car mechanics" (managers set up by the museum).[11]

In conclusion, I'd like to express my deepest appreciation for the opportunity to participate in these discussions that, in this particular moment in time, display a critical global need for museums to rethink their missions and gain new strategies in creating safe places and trusted social spaces that matter—museums that encourage their visitors to be not just spectators and observers but also participants in the ideas and questions that shape and protect our art, history, culture, and heritage, in the past and in the future.

NOTES

1. John H. Falk and Lynn D. Dierking, *Learning from Museums: Visitor Experiences and the Making of Meaning* (Walnut Creek, CA: AltaMira, 2000), 206.
2. Caroline Turner, "Editorial: Tomorrow's Museums," *Humanities Research* 8, no. 1 (2001): 1.
3. Hans-Martin Hinz, "Muzei—tse instrument prymyrennia suspilstva" (Museum is an instrument of social reconciliation), March 20, 2013 (Ukrainian).
4. Linda Norris, "If I Ran a Museum in Kyiv, Right Now," *Uncatalogued Museum*, December 1, 2013, http://uncatalogedmuseum.blogspot.com/2013/12/if-i-ran -museum-in-kyiv-right-now.html#.
5. Victoria Nuland quoted in Vysokyi Zamok, "Nuland: USA Back Participants of Euromaidan," December 17, 2013, http://wz.lviv.ua/news/48966-nuland -ssha-pidtrimuyut-uchasnikiv-evromajdanu (Ukrainian).
6. Maria Vlachou, "Museums 'For,' 'About,' and 'With' People," European Museum Advisors Conference, June 1, 2012, http://musingonculturextra.blogspot.pt/2012/06 /museum-for-about-and-with-people.html.
7. Gretchen Jennings, "Radical Open Authority: When Life Happens and Museums Respond," Museum Commons, December 17, 2013, http://www.museum commons.com/2013/12/radical-open-authority-when-life.html.
8. David Fleming, "Museums for Social Justice," 2014 American Alliance of Museums Annual Meeting and MuseumExpo.
9. Fiona Cameron, "Safe Places for Unsafe Ideas? History and Science Museums, Hot Topics and Moral Predicaments," *Social History in Museums* 32 (2008): 13–14.
10. Andrew Whitmarsh, "We Will Remember Them: Memory and Commemoration in War Museums," *Journal of Conservation and Museum Studies* 7 (2001): 11–15.
11. Ihor Poshyvailo, "Muzei Maidau: Bezpechne mistse dlia nebezbechnyh idei" (Maidan Museum: Safe place for unsafe ideas), *Muzeinyi prostir* 1, no. 11 (2014): 25 (Ukrainian).

Part Three

The Function
of Collecting

9

Why Do Museums Collect?

William Underwood Eiland

Heretofore, essential to the definition or even description of a museum was its collection. Of the other traits attributable to a museum, not surprisingly, were functions that aligned with or supported that collection: its preservation; the documentation of the objects or ephemera therein; research that both contextualized and demonstrated its meaning or value as representative of cultural, historic, or scientific heritage, both tangible and intangible; and its interpretation through exhibition and programming associated with its teaching and service missions.

In the search for an answer to the question "What is a museum?," one participant in a survey solicited by the International Council of Museums (ICOM) noted that collections are not limited to art, and that a museum is a "space where engagement with material culture and cultural ideas, values, heritage happens—space could be physical or virtual; engagement could be synchronous or asynchronous." Another participant took an almost spiritual view of the museum space as a "temple, hallowing sacred relics." And, making sure that "collections" encompass more than art, and exist in many types of museums, another respondent defined them as "group[s] of items, images, ideas, activities, animals, plants, specimens, etc., that educate, enlighten, entertain or illuminate aspects of that subject and promote further thought or discussion."

The function of collecting, given these considerations, therefore, is to increase or to refine the aggregate of objects, or even accompanying documents, that are organized, studied, and maintained in a museum, archive, library, or laboratory for the growth of knowledge of humankind's achievements as well as our failures. The function of collecting relates directly to the purpose embedded in a mission-centric museum's self-identity, as well as to its history, an element in the definition that goes well beyond tradition, heritage, or other positive characteristics alone.

Analyses of museums' collections reveal, often quite clearly, their roots in colonization, in complacency or indifference to the whole gamut of human accomplishment, and in elitist preoccupations, even unto obscurantism, that impede sharing the collection and its interpretation with audiences, too often limited to those patrons who are unintimidated or equipped with advance knowledge and less hesitant to enter the ivory towers that still seem to guard collections and constrain and marginalize some would-be visitors. In a pluralistic society, the museum and its collections, in the words of Danielle Kuijten, are the result of a "diaspora" of objects from their "communities of origin," but in deciding on restitution or repatriation, she is wary of not including in those discussions those living "close by and who also connect to these objects."[11]

Discussions of the role of collections in museum administration have centered on their growth, on their enhancement, or on their educational or scholarly value, but with the unsettling, decidedly discomfiting reality exposed by the Black Lives Matter movement and their own realization of inequities, museum professionals have looked with new foci, especially at collections, for those left out as much as those included. In order to rectify past indifference or, even more pointedly, neglect, to equitable treatment of the achievements of people of color, of Indigenous populations, of women and other groups ignored or unrepresented—and worse, misrepresented—museum practice finds itself under a high-intensity microscope, one that is revelatory of adherence to practice and standards no longer comprehensive or salutary for the present or the future.

What we collect, why we collect, and our management of those collections are global concerns, as relevant for museums in the Crimea as in the Andes. Even the Kunsthalle or gallery that only exhibits borrowed objects is not immune to these issues of inclusion in all its associated meanings of diversity, fairness, impartiality, and justice.

Of all the terms presented by those responding to ICOM's surveys of words and concepts to help in its new definition of "museum," "collections" and "collecting" were invariably mentioned as necessary to that meaning, as were certain functions such as conservation or interpretation. Linked now with more democratic ideals of representing all people, some responses coupled collecting with the colonizing past of museums, a new interpretation, perhaps, of a belief in the museum's "manifest destiny" in which institutions—judging their actions legitimate due to the perceived superiority of Western, Eurocentric traditions—often ruthlessly gathered, looted, or despoiled objects without regard to the cultural context of their origins. Museums are now and will in the future be questioning their colonial pasts and the avoidance of a neocolonial future. As the essays in this section clarify, the shared past of Western muse-

William Underwood Eiland

ums in particular calls for an investigation of their current practices as well as the existing collections for evidence of theft from Indigenous peoples, objects looted from archaeological sites, and purchases or acquisitions from dubious sources.

Tukufu Zuberi stresses the public nature of this discussion and emphasizes the museum as a space for such considerations of what it means to be a responsible citizen, especially in this case of local, regional, or national heritage and how to protect and steward it. He calls for a reevaluation of the role of museums in an open society, one that has too long supported a history of what he calls the "coloniality of Whiteness." In an indictment of museums for their complicity in this history, he calls them "repositories for the support of a Eurocentric interpretation of what it means to be a human being." His interpretation of decolonization is particularly appropriate in a discussion of collections and their presentation to the public, because for him each object has a narrative that must be investigated: where it originated, how it got into the museum, why it is being shown (or not shown), and whose material culture or history it represents. In the global search for new meaning, Zuberi's insights are critical, for he demonstrates his belief in the museum as a locus of civic virtue and belonging; his is, fittingly, the insight of a true internationalist.

This topic of the role of collecting—its function—in the modern and future museum is one that raises many more questions than it answers, which is the abiding theme of Kuijten's argument. Her point is that we must grapple with and answer the questions that are being posed as challenges; she finds that museums are literally "in survival mode," with increasing demands from our varied publics to "change, to face our historical selves, to diversify, and work more inclusively." For her, a pivotal role for museums is responding to the challenges posed by "finding new ways to redefine the meaning and practice of collecting." She stresses and describes her belief in heritage democracy, and in a purposeful double entendre, she advocates for "collective care" of our shared world heritage.[22]

Never far from the discussions of acquisition and management—as well as the individual museum's codes of ethics—is deaccessioning and the use of proceeds from the disposal of objects. The "bible" of art museums' practice in this regard has been *Professional Practices in Art Museums*, which clearly indicates that deaccessioning is a legitimate practice in refining a collection, but that proceeds from deaccessioning should only be used for reacquisition of objects that would carry the credit line of the donor of the original work, if applicable. In 2020, however, the Association of Art Museum Directors (AAMD), due to the threat to museums' human and fiscal resources by the COVID-19 pandemic, allowed for a limited time a moratorium of this prohibition such that funds could be used for the direct care of collections. The interpretation of that moratorium is the subject of Anne Pasternak's interview, in which she argues that proceeds from deaccessioning should be available for direct care of collections;

that rational thought about the issue reveals the fluidity of collections; and, equally important, that even though collections are "essential for many of our museums," they "are not the only consideration by any means." Perhaps most important in the discussion of the definition of "museum" is Pasternak's assertion that it is "high time to address the purpose of museums and what makes them meaningful and important." Describing herself as a "great believer in less storage, more galleries," for Pasternak, deaccessioning is indeed the elephant in the room and one unlikely to be liberated any time soon.

Regarding collection care, deaccessioning is an issue that has repercussions for other best practices in museums, with the highest standard from ICOM's current code of ethics:

> "Money or compensation received from the deaccessioning and disposal of objects and specimens from a museum collection should be used solely for the benefit of the collection and usually for acquisitions to that same collection." The adverbs in that policy are problematic, with "solely" descriptive rather than admonitory; and "usually" vague and ambiguous, especially because no definition is given regarding the phrase "for the benefit of the collection." Such lack of specificity is also responsible for part of the confusion over other associations' guidelines, particularly those that depend on a clear definition of "direct care" and even "public trust."

That issue is one that each museum as well as the peer professional associations to which it belongs is obligated to engage, due to the perils of unbridled deaccessioning for small, midsize, and academic museums. As Pasternak notes, the whole issue ties collection building and the care of collections to the issue of public trust. Thus, the museum must engage its audiences as well as its supporters in this discussion of the past and future of collecting. It should define for itself its role in the ethical acquisition and disposal of objects; its plan, if necessary, for repatriation of spoliated material; how it will engage a diverse public in the exhibition and interpretation of its collections; and the teaching function and how it is disseminated through scholarship of the collections. Each museum will be called upon to reconsider and answer these questions: What do we collect? How do we collect? Why do we collect? If the development of the collections is integral to the museum's mission, how does it handle deaccessioning and disposal, and does it have a recent analysis of its collection management policies as well as a detailed and transparent collecting plan? Notable in this discussion for museums in the United States is a nuance not applicable generally: it is a country that once was a colony of Great Britain, even though many of its museums' histories mirror or follow their European and even papal forerunners, at least in the creation of collections that, until the nineteenth century, remained private, generally only available to aristocrats or magnates.

Some radical commentators on this subject have a purist response to the value of collections in defining the "museum." They have argued in ICOM's polls and elsewhere that, because of the elitist quality of collections and their inherent nature as results of a colonialist past, their very existence should be questioned. The argument assumes that other materials and representations—reproductions or photographs—are sufficient in the arsenal of art history or criticism, that the reliance on objects themselves is obsolete, and that especially artifacts from archaeological digs should be left in situ so as not to disturb or confound "meaning" through the artificial medium of vitrine or diorama. The journalist Elisa Schoenberger has joined other thinkers, including Zuberi in this volume, in calling for an "overhauling of the entire system," not only to correct the injustices of the past but also to prepare for a more equitable future. Such an investigation of the origins of the current collection goes hand in glove with an analysis of the museum's functions of collecting, with attention to laws regarding the protection of cultural property. Some critics of museum practice also believe that connoisseurship as a method of studying objects in museums leads to the institution's "hoarding" knowledge or making access to it impenetrable.

Finally, regardless of the quality and quantity of its collections and their importance, perceived or evaluated, they do not entitle the museum to stand atop a pedestal, which should be reserved for the collection and its relationship with all the people who comprise our audiences and to whom we promise inspiration.

NOTES

1. "What Is a Museum? An Exploration in Six Parts; Part 2: The Function of Collecting," webinar, International Council of Museums, United States, https://www.icomus.org/webinar-series--part-two.
2. "What Is a Museum? Part 2."

10

KonMari in the Museum

COLLECTING FRONT, CENTER, AND BACK

Danielle Kuijten

PONDERINGS

This past year and a half, I have often found myself sitting at home with too much time spent on the internet. While scanning YouTube and Netflix, I finally started to check out the worldwide phenomenon of Marie Kondo, the decluttering guru. Consumed by thoughts on how to think differently about collecting and what has been collected and is kept in depots, I was in dire need of new insights. The appeal to look into Kondo was not so much about her KonMari method but more about the inspiration from which it was developed. So, I delved into that further.

I started to read up on Japanese minimalism, where mantras on keeping life simple, clean, and uncluttered are central; where the state of the lived environment also reflects the state of mind and vice versa. Another guru, Fumio Sasaki, is taking minimalist ideas much further than Kondo. He is seen as the example of the *Danshari* movement. Danshari is the Japanese word for "declutter," which consists of three kanji characters signifying refusal, disposal, and separation, translated into "cleaning up." The lines of thought behind this concept have religious dimensions derived from Zen Buddhism, which talks about the disposal of mental and physical burdens. These ideals speak not only of detachment from possessions but also refer to the detachment of passions and nonmaterial attachments. Today, it has become a true movement, or, depending on your mind-set, maybe just another fad, an avenue for new books and TV programs. This essay, however, is not about the minimalist movement, but about the all-consuming habit we seem to have evolved: collecting.

THE FRAME

Although the discussion on a new museum definition stirred up many emotions, the world came to a stop due to the pandemic. And while the pandemic seemed to paralyze us, a wave of protests quickly moved around the planet, trying to uproot certainties of the past. It questioned the status quo of public places, their narratives, and how public space is supposed to be for everyone but is not—how we have the same freedoms but also do not. How we are treated is the result of historically grown injustices. Internationally, the Black Lives Matter movement demanded attention for these wrongs that our societies maintain and have enforced for so long.

These different events—the definition, the pandemic, and the demonstrations—collided and brought common urgencies together about power relations, equity, and justice, which did not leave the museum untouched. For museums, as places where images are produced and reproduced, these urgencies were already part of larger discussions, but now, accountability and change have become more prominent.

COLLECTING

This is also why what has been collected, how it was collected, and how we proceed to collect are under heavy scrutiny—and as I see it, not without reason. It is, therefore, pivotal to reflect critically on the *evidence*, the *sources*, and the created and used *knowledge systems*. By doing so, we can uncover layers

Figure 10.1. Semipermanent showcase: Collecting/Collectables—Memories/Memorabilia. © *Les Adu | Imagine IC, 2019*

of social, political, cultural, scientific, and individual power relations. Trying to understand these power relations and the meaning-making process of collecting is key. It not only creates awareness of our actions in the past and makes visible their significance for communities or society at large but it also makes us all accountable for what we do with the new information and how we enforce change.

By revisiting historical narratives in general as well as that of collections, and through contemporary collecting or documenting the present, we seek new meanings—by trying to create space for social memories, unhide the hidden, and write what has been left out so far. In these trajectories, we should not forget to also revisit the language and choice of words we use and the labels that have been created. If we talk about objects as evidence, what do we mean by that? And if it's not there, does that mean evidence is missing, or does it not exist? Evidence and proof for whom? To what purpose?

One major concern is omission, whether this is determined by politics, professional ethics, the law, or social agenda. How did and do curators collect? How does the political context affect the collected? How can museums collect from groups that seem to "deviate" from society's norms? By adapting to and reflecting the world around it, the collection aims to continue to challenge and acknowledge its historical roots. New acquisitions are considered by subject, theme, or an artist's personal experience, all of which resonate with different aspects of contemporary society.

In my work, I have been thinking about how we, in museums and heritage institutions, can use complexity and subjectivity as a means to narrate and listen to each other. What happens if we provide multiple voices, add new significances, and work nonhierarchically? In other words: What happens if we change institutionally controlled narratives to ones where the objects are disconnected from explicit explanations and linked laterally to multivaried avenues of exploration? And how do we deal with that in a sustainable manner?

Activities such as selecting, collecting, discarding, and arranging attribute social value to the chosen objects. When being musealized, the object, as well as having artistic, scientific, or patrimonial value, becomes an actor within a social network. In *Unpacking the Collection: Networks of Material and Social Agency in the Museum*, the authors discuss "new ways to think about the relationship formed between object and individuals and among diverse groups spread across the globe."[1]

The museological object is not something passive. Sherry Turkle wrote about this in the introduction to her book *Evocative Objects. Things We Think With*, from 2007: "Objects can be emotional and intellectual companions that anchor memory, sustain relationships and provoke new ideas."[2] It is the museum's duty to maintain certain dynamics, making sure that new meanings, emotions, and relations, with regard to the objects and collections, will be added and preserved.

Currently, the practice of collecting as a *traditional*, key function of museums seems under threat in the bigger discussion of what the museum is and does. Should collecting remain in its position for the future, and what should collecting entail?

THE CONVERSATION

As chair of COMCOL, ICOM's International Committee on Collecting, but also from my position at Imagine IC, the contemporary challenges *in* and perspectives *on* collecting and collections are at the core of my work and, therefore, very much intertwined. Although museums are still in survival mode as a result of the global pandemic, we cannot forget the previous pressing challenge, one that remained strongly vocalized during the past year and will continue for the foreseeable future. This search gives shape to the urgent requests from society to make a change, face our historical selves, and diversify and work more inclusively.

We have to tackle various issues connected to the idea of the museum, with collections taking a pivotal role. Change has begun, though not with a much-needed open mind-set, organizationally deep dedication, or necessary critical self-reflection and transparency. Within this turmoil, we are also trying to find a new definition for museums at the heart of this series from ICOM-US. My personal quest is finding new ways to redefine the meaning and practice

Figure 10.2.   Opening exhibition memorializing the Bijlmer disaster. © *Les Adu* | *Imagine IC, 2017*

Danielle Kuijten

of collecting and inviting my colleagues all over the world not to act and react within their practice out of habit but critically reflect on what has been done and question how we can make necessary changes. It is for that reason that I started the so-called co-collection lab in 2016 at Imagine IC.

As a participatory organization located in a highly diverse part of town for the past twenty years, we work on concepts of heritage democracy. We are, for many bigger institutions, the go-to in order to gain access to our networks. But we refrain from being just a Rolodex with contacts in our partnerships. When institutions work with us, they must fully commit and engage with the networks to find new understandings of heritage work. With partners such as the Amsterdam City Archives, the Tropenmuseum (part of the Museum of World Cultures), the Amsterdam Museum, and the Museum Van Loon, to name but a few, we discuss different questions on collecting and collections.

These institutional partners are not only having these discussions with us and each other, but more important, also with people from our neighborhood network—with participants who come to us with personal stories, archives, and objects. To us, they are as much experts at the table as anybody else. During the sessions, we look at balancing the interests, importance, and expectations of institutional and private participants. We talk about the process of collecting, the requirements under which objects are obtained, and from that moment, the circumstances under which they can or cannot be shown, how selections are made, and the narratives told. Questions of safeguarding for future generations, as opposed to accessibility for the current generation, are also addressed. What existing hierarchies are in place around ownership and authority? How does institutional expert knowledge oppose knowledge based on personal experience or oral traditions?

So, what are the ethics of collecting we abide by? And whose ethics are they? For the past three years, we have had a canoe from Ghana in-house—an object from the Tropenmuseum that had never been exhibited nor was planned to be. In sessions with participants beforehand, we found out this canoe represented a sense of home to many. We then decided to negotiate whether the canoe could come to us, close to those connected to it. This came with some challenges: our building is not climatized, and we share it with the public library—and, on paper, there were many more reasons not to approve such a move. But it was decided that the object was of greater value within our district than locked away in a depot.

Over the coming years, we will take part in a big national project called Pressing Matters, Ownership, Value, and the Question of Colonial Heritage in Museums, headed by the Museum of World Cultures and the Vrije Universiteit Amsterdam. This national research tries to go beyond questions about where colonial objects came from and to whom they belong by also exploring for whom they carry meaning today. And where is this meaning most relevant? At Imagine IC, we will look at the different homes that both humans and objects embody—how to look, consider, and work with the concept of multiple homes. Neither here nor there, or here and there. And what happens in the in-between space.

For me, this rethinking and searching for new ideas on collecting and collections is also visible in the transformation of wording from the current definition to the one proposed in Kyoto. The current definition reads, "The museum acquires, conserves, researches, communicates and exhibits the tangible and intangible heritage of humanity and its environment." The proposed version is formulated differently: "Museums are participatory and transparent and work in active partnership with and for diverse communities to collect, preserve, research, interpret, exhibit and enhance understandings of the world." The difference to me is in *collect* as opposed to *acquire*. You can consider this semantics, which it is, and exactly what we need in this discussion: being word-sensitive.

How can we use our collections and practices of collecting to understand contemporary societies and find ways to shape our futures together? How can we rethink what safeguarding means, what ownership entails, and how passing ownership on or returning acts of care can be formulated? How can we be open to listening to others, critically reflect on how things were done in the past, and better this? For me, collecting is identifying, sharing, temporarily holding onto to show, researching in togetherness, and leaving things in situ. So how can collecting become an act of collective care in which the human, not the object, is at the center?

NOTES

1. Sarah Byrne, Anne Clarke, Rodney Harrison, and Robin Torrence, *Unpacking the Collection: Networks of Material and Social Agency in the Museum* (New York: Springer, 2011), 3.
2. Sherry Turkle, *Evocative Objects: Things We Think With* (Cambridge, MA: MIT Press, 2007), 5.

11

On Museums and Collecting

Kate Quinn with Anne Pasternak

Since 2015, Anne Pasternak has served as the Shelby White and Leon Levy director of the Brooklyn Museum, one of the oldest and largest fine arts institutions in the nation. For more than thirty years, Anne has devoted her career to engaging broad audiences with the limitless power of art to move, motivate, and inspire.

The following excerpt stems from the webinar series "What Is a Museum? An Exploration in Six Parts." The series explored the role of museums in society in light of the discussions surrounding a new definition of "museum," and this conversation focused on the function of collection. We asked four questions of Anne regarding her thoughts on collections and collecting practices in museums today.

Kate Quinn: As a staunch advocate for the civic and democratic roles of our cultural and educational institutions, you are committed to projects that demonstrate the crucial links between art and social justice, so let me ask, what should be the role of collections within a new definition of museums?

Anne Pasternak: It's an important question. Museum mission statements have historically stated that museums collect, preserve, care for, interpret, and share collections. But we also know that many great museums don't have collections. The truth of the matter is, museums have a bigger purpose: We are rare places in public life in which people can come together, learn, share, debate, imagine, and inspire. Whether or not a museum is a collecting institution, this is our greater collective mission. And it's a critically important role as we become increasingly divided politically, economically, even digitally.

63

Quinn: Some of those divisions revolve around deaccessioning collections—if to do so, when to do so, and why. Although not a new topic, it has gained more public traction in recent months. Many agree that to be a museum, an institution must have a collection. What are your thoughts on this?

Pasternak: Deaccessioning is a hot topic in our field and in the global media—it always is. Recently the Brooklyn Museum began deaccessioning artworks to raise $40 million for the ongoing, permanent care of our collections—one of the most important functions of any collecting museum. Deaccessioning is not new. Museums have been deaccessioning since their founding. It's not new for us at the Brooklyn Museum, either, though most of deaccessioning has been focused on gifting works to educational institutions and repatriations, especially Native American repatriations.

Sales have been much less frequent and have been done for the sole purpose of creating much-needed acquisition funds at the Brooklyn Museum. We still need larger acquisitions funds, but with direct costs rising exponentially over the past two decades, and with more than two dozen overflowing storage rooms in the museum, it was clear that important resources were being spent on less important works. It was high time to begin refining the collection, keeping the best, and raising funds to cover the essential expenses related to the "direct care" of all our great works.

The Brooklyn Museum has more than 160,000 objects in its collection, and works recently deaccessioned constitute less than 0.001 percent of the collection. Many of these works are very good, but they were not our best. Most had not been exhibited for decades and some not ever. In some cases, we had far stronger examples in the collection for which we are better known; others were just outliers in our collection. Once the museum has attained its collections' care goal, we will continue to deaccession to raise needed funds for acquisitions and to free up storage to create more galleries. I'm a big believer in less storage, more galleries.

It might surprise you to know that I'm fairly conservative in matters of deaccessioning, as I love objects and I hate to let anything go. I understand concerns about deaccessioning, but I'd argue it's time to rethink museum orthodoxies because we are—and we ought to be—more than static repositories for art. Collections have always been more fluid than the field acknowledges. The truth is, deaccessions can strengthen a collection through refinements, right-sizing a collection, and addressing historic collection errors and oversights. Let us not forget that museums such as the Brooklyn Museum acquired vast holdings in the twentieth century without a clear, strong strategy for accepting gifts. Deaccessioning can correct errors of the past and support the future.

Plus, we just can't accumulate endlessly. We've never had the financial support to properly sustain such a large and growing collection and fulfill other mission-critical activities. What good are we if we are object rich but cash poor—too poor to care for our collections, interpret, study, and even show them? It is sometimes said that deaccessioning is a violation of the public trust. I get that, but the ability to carry out our mission—and achieve its greatest potential—is also an issue of public trust. The ability to care for our collection is an issue of public trust. So, it's time to openly and honestly discuss the realities and complexities of caring for collections. It's time to address the purpose of museums and what makes them meaningful and important. And it's time to discuss what it means to "care." Yes, collections are essential for many of our museums, but they are not the *only* consideration.

Quinn: Let's talk about the concept of rethinking museum orthodoxies. Should museums be more than a repository for art and objects?

Pasternak: Many great museums have no collections at all, so clearly museums are more than a repository for art. At our very basic essence, we are places of learning, gathering, creation, and inspiration through art. But a lot of ideas that we've held to be tried and true about museums are worth questioning, especially at this time when we are faced with so many challenges—from the impact of digital platforms to contending with the field's unethical practices. It's healthy, even necessary, to question the orthodoxies. I came to the Brooklyn Museum not having run a museum before. So, I questioned everything. I'm sure that was very irritating to my team, but it was also powerful in helping us think about what we were doing and why we were doing it. It has helped us better use our resources and align them with our values. It helped us shape a stronger collection and exhibitions strategy. It helped us grow educational reach and audience size. And it helped us deepen community impact and expand our DEIA commitments in structural, meaningful ways.

Audiences are calling on us to change. The data supports that more and more people believe in the importance of museums, but they want us to tell inclusive, truthful histories and to be pillars of good for our society. All around the globe, cultural institutions have been busy reinventing themselves to meet the rapidly changing demands of the day. Adapting to the reality that people can download books for free on their phones, the Brooklyn Public Library system has evolved from buildings with books to places of learning and civic participation. The Wildlife Conservation Society doesn't just provide places to see animals, at the Bronx Zoo and the New York Aquarium; it's a globally powerful organization meeting the challenges of capitalism and environmental devastation through education and policy change around the world. These are just a few of the great cultural institutions that have looked at how the world is changing and adapted to meet the challenges head-on. They questioned long-held orthodoxies and, as a result, they are realizing the greater potential of their missions. It's time museums did the same.

Quinn: In a world aimed toward political correctness, how do we address collections as a result of power and colonization? Should our collections shift as our communities do?

Pasternak: Is the world aimed toward political correctness? I'm not sure. . . . But it is clear that many museum collections are inextricably linked to power and colonization. For example, the Brooklyn Museum's creation, nearly two hundred years ago, grew out of the desire to compete with the great cultural institutions in Europe and the United Kingdom, as a way to promote and celebrate the growing power of our new nation. Though the great "encyclopedic" collections overseas were created through vast royal wealth, trade, conquest, and colonization, U.S. museums such as the Brooklyn Museum mirrored their ideologies and practices. Although I firmly believe that it is important to uphold the greater importance of our missions to care for and share the great cultural traditions of the world, audiences are also right to call on museums to acknowledge the complexities and complicities of our practices. At the Brooklyn Museum, we are responding through many measures, including in-gallery interpretation that acknowledges our past, policies that improve provenance practices, and repatriation for works wrongfully acquired.

Our collecting strategies are also shifting to respond to the changing times. For example, the Brooklyn Museum is in central Brooklyn, where we have a very strong Caribbean population, but we don't have a strong Caribbean collection. That's something we are addressing because it's essential that we do better in celebrating the great cultural traditions of our neighbors.

At the same time, I think it is healthy to consider why and whether we maintain some of our other collections. For example, we call ourselves an encyclopedic museum, but we certainly are not encyclopedic—we are a mishmash of great works from around the world, with our strongest collections in Egyptian, African, American, European, and Asian art. Whole parts of art history from around the globe are missing, and we have collections that have never had a dedicated curator and have rarely, if ever, been on view. Should we keep those collections? Or should we deaccession them to support things of greater importance to present and future audiences? These are hard and complex questions, but ones worth addressing.

This is a revolutionary time for our field. Why wouldn't it be? It's a revolutionary time in the world, as we witness vast migrations, environmental devastation, and political divisiveness. Either we lean in, or we do our institutions and our audiences a great disservice. This is a moment to reach for the greatest potential of our missions. This is a time to ask what we stand for. When we look back at our lives and our service to this field, will we look back with pride? Did we contribute to greater decency and opportunity for people? Or did we promote narratives and structures that upheld the law of white supremacy and diminished and harmed others? This is a reckoning. It's long overdue.

12

Beyond Colonial Collecting

Tukufu Zuberi

The museum can be an important place for public conversation, public consideration, and discourse on how to be a responsible citizen. It is an essential institution for nations and peoples in giving definition to who they are. I mean, the idea of having 850 million visits per year (in the pre-COVID period) places the museum at the center of the public debate about who we are.

This is an important moment, and in the summer of 2020, the youth-led Black Lives Matter movement declared "enough is enough." This is an important moment because, on January 6, 2021, a confederate flag flew in the Capitol of the United States. As a result, we have had to reconsider how we do things, where we do things, and how we organize public spaces. This is an important moment to reconsider the role of the museum. Museums themselves in the West (whether in the United States or in Europe) have functioned as a way of rearticulating the coloniality of Whiteness. They have been the repositories to support a Eurocentric interpretation of what it means to be a human being.

Now, many museums have been created with the direct purpose of challenging this foundation and taking us beyond this place. Museums such as the African American Museum of History and Culture in the United States, Museu-Afro Brasil, and Senegal's Musée des Civilisations Noires were all created to challenge this narrative of white supremacy at both the national and international levels. And many of the major museums around the world are having conversations about how to change in response to this new ground. And this new ground is one where inclusion and diversity are essential. At the same moment that we have the Black Lives Matter movement, we also have the rise of white supremacist articulations of taking America back to a point when it was not great—rather than looking forward to a moment when it could achieve greatness. Museums can serve a very important role in this process.

And I think that a lot of the debate around decolonization, decolonizing the museum, decolonizing the collections of museums, and decolonizing the perspectives of museums is essential. Because it's not only an issue of having the power to display objects; it is also the narrative around those objects themselves. How did they get to the museums? Why are museums showing them or not showing them? What does this create in terms of our understanding of who we are as human beings? And who are the people represented by these pieces of material culture? Whether it is a piece of art that is just there for our appreciation or a bronze sculpture of an Oba from the Benin Kingdom that has religious significance, its cultural importance is worthy of our consideration. We need to appreciate the significance of how such a key cultural object ends up in a museum in Germany, Paris, New York, or Philadelphia.

I am excited about this moment because it is one in which we can challenge the messaging that comes from this institution, which should serve a leading role in questioning our humanity and our citizenship. These conversations should be taking place in the galleries. They are taking place in a lot of ways. Sometimes the conversation consists of responding to the creative impulses of the communities in your locality. At other times, it is by responding to the creative impulses of people around the globe as they challenge what it means to be a human being.

Many people were shocked when the marches took place during the summer of the Black Lives Matter movement in the United States. It was taken up as a challenge by people in Hong Kong, London, Paris, and Lagos, Nigeria. But this is the world we live in today. It is a world in which intercommunication around the globe is engaged. The circulation of information is continuously ongoing, and what role do we play in that process? I always feel when I'm working on a project in a museum that we must challenge ourselves to go further. We must challenge the museum itself, the practice of museology. We must challenge what the space has done and what it portends to do in the future.

TRANSFORMING THE NARRATIVE

I really do believe we're at a very important moment when, in August 2019, the *New York Times* published the "1619 Project," and we get a response to it in the "1776 Report," released on Martin Luther King Jr. Day in 2021. I mean, if you think about it, the museum can provide a venue for this conversation. And it would be easy for me to dismiss one side of this argument, but I think it is necessary to have the conversation in order to support education.

I've worked in very different kinds of museums—I've had things exhibited and curated things in various types of institutions— it's given me a sensitivity to the fact that not all museums are trying to do the same thing. And through that, I could see the operational ends that people are engaged with. But then there's the larger mission of museums themselves, and I think this is the space in which public education, public conversation, and public debate should take place. The issue about whether it's 1619 or 1776, and what the significance of those dates offers us—in terms of understanding the importance of the legacy of enslavement or coloniality in the United States—and what that has meant to how we present history and culture—can be openly addressed.

For the most part, museums have done the work of helping the hijacked interpretation of white supremacy—whether it is white supremacy coming out of Paris, Humboldt, New York, Washington, or wherever. But a fundamental response has been taking place. You might say that you can see it happening with the Harlem Renaissance. You can see it happening with Negritude. You can see it happening with the various Pan-African Congresses responding to and rejecting the cultural interpretation of Africa, which limits our view of the humanity of Africans, much less Black people in Brazil, Colombia, and the United States, because those definitions are all entwined with each other.

The museum can be a force of enlightenment, or it can return to those days when it helped put a shadow over knowledge and information. It's not like these places didn't have history; it's not like a bronze of an Oba's face doesn't have significance in Benin. But another spiritual significance happens when you rip it out of that context and put it in a museum in Philadelphia. And you don't undo that by simply giving it back. I was talking to a museum director in Senegal recently about this idea of repatriating restituted objects, and he said, "Well, to think about many of these objects, they do have this soul."

And what happens to the soul of an object that is stolen, put in a place, and misinterpreted for many years? Where does that narrative begin to find some way of healing? And that, to me, suggests that this cross-cultural circulation, which was facilitated by imperialism, can be interrupted by us introducing a different kind of cross-cultural conversation with those museums—building bonds, so that the story is told in a way that it needs to be told. The stories of the Benin cultures and Edo culture need to be recounted in the United States. But they also need to be understood within the context of this material culture representing this part of current-day Nigeria.

In the end, the museum should be providing information to improve the quality of the conversations we are having in public about who we are, what our world is, and what we can do in this world.

SHIFTING HOW MUSEUMS COLLECT

The museum, as a practice, originated during the time of enslavement and colonialism. The objective of museums, therefore, is encased within this societal mission. It's not like you can escape that, and you can't escape the interpretations that have followed this colonial logic. That's why we're calling for decolonizing the narrative in museums—even if it's the sculptures from Greece in the British Museum. In all of this, we need to have a different conversation about what is being collected, why it's being collected, and what purpose it can serve in these social conversations. Racism is an essential component of colonialism, and it is an essential component of enslavement.

If you look at African objects—especially classical and historical African objects—all of them were made or collected during the period of enslavement and colonialism. And so, to see or discuss the restitution of these objects, you need to be talking about racism and about those diaspora populations in Germany, France, Paris, Brazil, and the United States.

This is the nature of the conversation. We should be enlightening people about what has really happened. There's no need for us to be ashamed of the colonial past—it created anthropology, Egyptology, and sociology. All of these disciplines have the same colonial mentality that we need to decolonize, as well. We have a good mission here. Let's take it.

This change in objective should lead to a shift in how museums collect objects. I think we can talk about this shift in two ways. One way is to talk about the shift in objects, the shift in what is presented. Another is to talk about a shift in the narrative. These conversations happen, and in artwork, they happen: artists are inspired by each other, by what's going on in the world, and sometimes their narratives cut across the pieces they're engaged in. Material culture, as it represents something in a particular place, has this ability to engage in a conversation. I'll give you one example so I can make my final point.

If you take a Christian cross from Angola, you might say it was created because of an impact of Portuguese colonialism in Angola, or something like that. If you take a cross from Egypt or Ethiopia, you might say that this cross influenced how they made crosses in Rome because they had been making crosses there a little bit longer than in Europe. There we get two different views about the spread of Christianity from these different spaces in Africa: one being where Christianity is thought to have arrived *from* Europe, and the other that is known to have contributed a great amount of material culture and iconography *to* Christianity in Europe. The objects are essentially the same, yet the narrative about their social significance in understanding our "now" and thinking about the roots of Christianity could play a different role in the museum.

It's not just the things themselves; it's also how we talk about them. We need to elevate the conversation. And in many places, this will mean that you might have one thing, but you need another thing in order to talk about the first one you collected. It might mean that you have an object, but you need a relationship with the place from where it came. It may not be enough to have a bunch of objects that represent Yoruba culture and have no connection with Yoruba people, as they are continuing to evolve their culture—whether in Cuba, Brazil, or Nigeria. Understanding our job means that we need to be on the side of comprehending the complexity of what we do, what we have, and what it represents.

I agree with this idea of responding to the presence of people who have been ignored until this point in our community—there's no question. Renata Felinto is the artist of the series *Don't Count on the Fairy*. In it, she is working through some issues about the impact of fairy tales on the identity formation of non-European children—in relation to phenotype, acceptance of one's own image, and attitudes in social life in Brazil. The fairy-tale atmosphere of these stories is fused with images of Black girls. Now, what role do these artworks serve to educate people in the United States about what it means to be a girl here, compared to what it means to be a girl there? I don't pretend to know the answers to that, but I do know that it is a question we should be asking. And it's only by having works like this in these spaces that we begin to have these conversations.

Figure 12.1.   Renata Felinto, Untitled, part of *Don't Count on the Fairy*, 2011. Acrylic, gouache, dry pastel, stickers, and appliqué on card, 72 × 50 cm. *Courtesy Tukufu Zuberi Collection, Philadelphia, PA*

Figure 12.2. Renata Felinto, Untitled, part of *Don't Count on the Fairy*, 2011. Acrylic, gouache, dry pastel, stickers, and appliqué on card, 72 × 50 cm. *Courtesy Tukufu Zuberi Collection, Philadelphia, PA*

Figure 12.3. Renata Felinto, Untitled, part of *Don't Count on the Fairy*, 2011. Acrylic, gouache, dry pastel, stickers, and appliqué on card, 72 × 50 cm. *Courtesy Tukufu Zuberi Collection, Philadelphia, PA*

That, to me, is an important role for the museum to have. But it also shows how material culture should not be fetishized in a way that disconnects it from the people who produce the culture. These objects, these things, were created by people—unless it is just a rock you picked up and brought from somewhere. And I can dig that, too. Or a dinosaur you simply reassembled somewhere (I can dig that as well). But, if you're talking about the things that represent human material culture, you need to connect that to the people—the people from whom these things came. And in the case of the African objects taken from the continent during this period or represented, you have to not only connect to the people from Africa but also to these diasporas that you find here.

That's why I use the example of the Yoruba. Yoruba culture is spread all over the world; it's not only grounded in Nigeria. It is necessary to understand that if you want to understand the culture of Cuba, Brazil, Haiti, or New Orleans. This is a way of taking the complexities of the intersections of information and knowledge and offering them to the people so their small community, which they think is only them, begins to see how it's connected to all of us.

Part Four

The Whiteness
of Museums

13

Assymetries of Power

MUSEUMS AND WHITENESS

Lyndel King

Museums are undergoing an effort to acknowledge and recognize with concern the legacies and continuous presence of deep societal inequalities and asymmetries of power and wealth globally, nationally, regionally, and locally. How could museums reverse their lineage and attain diversity in a continuous, organic fashion?

Museums, as we think of them today, were, from the beginning, White, elitist institutions. Although archaeologists have uncovered evidence that public display of collections may have occurred in what is now southern Iraq as early as 530 BC, modern museums are basically a product of the Enlightenment movement, which dominated the world of ideas in Europe in the late seventeenth and eighteenth centuries.

The word "museum" comes from Ancient Greek and refers to the "seat of muses." It was used to describe places for philosophical discussions. In the fifteenth century, the collection of Lorenzo de' Medici in Italy was sometimes described as a museum. "Museum" also sometimes referred to a private collection of curiosities brought together by wealthy individuals lusting to acquire incredible artifacts, natural and man-made, from around the world. These precursors of the modern museum were called cabinets of curiosities because of the eclectic nature of the collections—from natural history specimens to scientific wonders to cultural and religious artifacts.

Others may contend for the distinction of being the world's first public museum, but the Ashmolean at Oxford University in England usually claims this title. Elias Ashmole gave his collection of curiosities to the University of Oxford, and a special building to house it opened to the public in 1683. The museum became a repository for rare materials and a center for research and learning for the elite of England and Western Europe.

Thus, the beginnings of the modern museum were steeped in the European Enlightenment's emphasis on reason and rigorous scientific, political, and philosophical discourse. Exploration and scientific experimentation went hand in hand. Cultures and people outside the European center were considered merely the subjects for this research and exploration. The superiority of White Europeans was implicit in this endeavor.

From this beginning, European—and later, American—museums and educational institutions evolved. University education is no longer for an elite group of White students. Or is it? Today, museums in America and Europe are very different places. Or are they?

Enlightenment thinking, which strongly influenced the United States' founding fathers, argued that liberty was a human right, and reason and scientific knowledge were responsible for human progress. But this reliance on "science" included a rationale for slavery, based on a hierarchy of races. The idea that all the species of the world, including human beings, could be classified and ordered flourished during the Enlightenment. Just as the Swedish botanist Carl Linnaeus's publication in 1753 is considered the true beginning of plant taxonomy, Enlightenment thinker Johann Friedrich Blumenbach's 1776 volume *On the Natural Varieties of Mankind* categorizes humans. The German philosopher Immanuel Kant wrote about egalitarian principles, yet used science to justify sexism, racism, and slavery. In his later years, he criticized European colonialism and slavery, but his views on the classification of the races, with White males at the top because of their perceived superior ability to reason and think abstractly, were in line with other thinkers of his time.

In this context of a worldview based on reason, science, and experimentation supporting racist and sexist ideas, Western museums emerged. So, in the West, including the United States, museums were White from the beginning and have remained that way for much of the ensuing centuries.

The cabinets of curiosities of the sixteenth century, out of which many European museums emerged, were formed with the idea of collections that produced wonder in the viewer, who could see natural and cultural phenomena from around the world. They were seen as places for scientific study—as well as tools to establish the social rank for their owners. Ashmole, described as a "true Enlightenment polymath," gave his cabinet of curiosities to Oxford University with the proviso that a separate building open to the public be constructed to house it. "His vision was to create a center for practical research and the advancement of knowledge of the natural world."[1] One may assume that most, if not all, of the students at Oxford University in 1683, when the Ashmolean Museum was established, were White, male, and from the nobility or were the sons of the clergy and wealthy merchant class.

Arising from this milieu, it would have been difficult for museums in Europe and the United States to be anything but White in their outlook. Although collections may have included artifacts representing many different cultures, those were seen primarily as "specimens" to be studied by the superior race of White scientists and students. Some came from the explorations during the so-called Age of Exploration from the fourteenth through sixteenth centuries. And many objects in museums were undoubtedly loot accumulated as a result of Western nations' colonization, particularly in the Americas, Africa, and India in the centuries after those regions' "discovery" by White Europeans.

Painter Charles Willson Peale's Cabinet of Curiosities in Philadelphia, which opened in 1786, is often cited as one of the first museums in the United States. Some sources cite the 1773 founding of a museum by the Charleston Library Society in Charleston, South Carolina, as the first museum in the United States, but most acknowledge Peale's as the first public museum. Many significant museums in Europe were founded at about that time, such as the British Museum in London in 1759 and the Louvre in Paris in 1793. The first big museum boom came at the beginning of the nineteenth century with a realization of the role of the museum in contributing to national consciousness. In the United States, the museum boom came later; at least 75 percent of museums in the United States were founded after 1950 and 40 percent of those after 1970.[2]

Thus, Whiteness emerges at the foundation of many if not all museums in Europe and the United States, particularly those early, prestigious institutions. It has continued to this day.

Major European museums are funded mainly by governments, but in the United States museums receive the majority of their funding from private donors. This fact has required American museums to cater to the interests of these privileged, and primarily White, groups in their collections, programming, and operations.

Museums have grasped at a few significant areas of change to atone for their past Whiteness and to respond to the world of today, which is much different from the world into which they were born. One is to diversify their staffs and boards of directors. When the Black Lives Matter movement reached a fever pitch in summer 2020, most museums still had only a small number of Black, Indigenous, and people of color (BIPOC) on their staffs and boards.[3] The reasons for this are not to be found in the racism of individual museum leaders but in the structural racism that is so much part of the conversation today. I imagine that American museum directors see themselves as progressive and nonracist. For many years at museum association meetings, they have bemoaned the dearth of people of color on their staffs and boards. People of color have generally entered the museum profession as curators and directors of ethnic-specific museums and departments. A few have now moved into the larger museum field, but they are still relatively rare.

The reasons for this are complex and intertwined. Museums in the United States, formed with the collections of wealthy White people, still receive much of their financial support from that group. Early museum curators and directors—usually White men—often came from families that could support their career in the museum field, given the relatively low salaries the positions paid. That has changed as more middle-class men and women have moved into museum positions. Today, museum leaders understand the value of having a diverse staff and say they want to hire more people of color. However, many museum positions still require a relatively high level of education, even if that level of education doesn't necessarily correlate to doing the job well.

Museum executives consistently blame the "pipeline" for not producing people of color with qualifications to assume specialized curatorial positions that can lead to the executive office. Museum positions generally require an expensive education but do not offer equally high remuneration, particularly for entry-level positions. For this reason, BIPOC students and their families may not embrace the idea of a museum career.

Museum curators and directors tend to come from families that have achieved a certain status that allows their children to "embrace their passions." As an immigrant student or first in the family to attend college, a degree in business, law, or medicine may be much more appealing than spending the same money to educate oneself for a position in a museum that offers a fraction of the salary of those other professions. Thus, the high cost of education today is detrimental to attracting a diverse pool of applicants for museum positions.

Nearly every museum in the United States, whether large or small, focused on art or science or natural history, talks about the need to decolonize or restructure itself to be free from the Whiteness of its foundation and even more recent history. Museums want to see themselves as agents of change and as responsive to their communities. The COVID-19 pandemic has forced many museums to cut staff to survive financially. But even those museums that have made drastic changes as a way to stabilize finances have been quick to make points such as, in the case of the Oakland Museum of California: "The restructuring . . . is in part being carried out with the intent of rendering the museum an anti-racist and equitable multicultural institution . . . more relevant to our community and . . . consistent with our vision for our social impact."[4] Whether this will bear out is yet to be seen.

Museums have also begun to address Whiteness in their collections. In the late 1980s, the Guerrilla Girls, an anonymous group of female artists, exposed discrimination against women artists in the art museum world. Since then, the exposure of racist and sexist practices, particularly in art museums, has snowballed. This may be because, for the most part (leaving aside the multimillions that major science museums have paid for crowd-pleasing dinosaur skeletons), art museum collections are where the money is.

The thorny issue of deaccessioning in art collections to acquire works by BIPOC artists has made the news, including the Baltimore Museum of Art's plan to sell several significant artworks to "achieve equity both in its collection and staff. Funds from the sales would be distributed among several initiatives, including ones meant to diversify the museum's holding with works by women and artists of color."[5] Even though the sale was called off at the last minute, the furor it aroused on both sides of the issue remains. For museums with small acquisition budgets, as is the case in many smaller regional and academic museums, a collection more responsive to its community's changing demographics is tough to achieve.

Museums have not yet come to any agreement on whether their "permanent collections" are truly permanent or whether they are disposable to allow museums to be more responsive to the current pressures of the society in which they exist. Should art museums abandon the idea of permanence in their collections and be free to sell collections in order to diversify staff? Should they sell their acknowledged masterpieces by White artists to purchase more works by BIPOC artists? How do art museums, particularly, deal with the fact that most of their acquisitions come as gifts or bequests, not purchases? In 2015, the Association of Art Museum Directors reported that 85 percent of additions to the collection came through gifts or bequests.[6] Although some enlightened collectors have begun to respond by adding more artists of color to their collections, many opt for the tried-and-true old masters. With their financial well-being depending on individual donors, how do American museums walk the tightrope between not wanting to insult their donors while at the same time remaining true to their diversity goals?

These questions are not answered definitively and are the subject of much discussion in the museum world. The answers will require skilled museum leadership and responsive donors.

Another primary response of museums to the new world in which they operate is to reexamine their approach to interpretation. Science and natural history museums must respond to the ecological concerns of patrons and staff alike. Museums must address the perilous state of our planet, and natural history and science museums are in a perfect place to undertake this education. They can help educate the public about the actions that must be taken if our way of living on Earth is to be salvaged. These museums are refurbishing their exhibitions and reinterpreting their collections toward this essential educational goal.

Art and history museums are in the best position to address social issues through their collections and exhibitions. Artist/curators such as Fred Wilson have helped reinterpret collections with projects such as his groundbreaking 1992–1993 installation *Mining the Museum* at the Maryland Historical Society in Baltimore. He placed articles from the collection in startling juxtaposition, such as iron slave shackles next to a silver vessel and a whipping post next to

Victorian chairs. This installation unsettled the comfortable narrative of up-per-class life in the region by drawing attention to the local histories of Black and Indigenous people. Although some viewers were hostile, suggesting that the show would promote violence among people of color, most viewers were profoundly moved and reported positive life-changing and view-changing experiences.[7]

Art and history museums are moving beyond the special exhibition to carry out their social responsibility. They are digging deeper into the provenance of their collections to include sometimes uncomfortable details of their collection history as part of their interpretations. They are looking beyond the traditional art historical or mainstream historical context to reveal different histories and different contexts.

Still, the work is far from over.

Museums, especially large, well-established ones, are not known for nim-bleness. At the same time, the world may not let museums rest. Museum staff activists, artists, ecologists, and a growing number of ordinary citizens demand that these institutions catch up and respond to their communities that are changing rapidly partly because of demographic shifts in the population of the United States. The clock cannot be turned back. Demographics of communities are changing whether or not museums are ready. Museums in Europe and the United States cannot deny their essential Whiteness, nor can they undo it. They can go forward with clear eyes and a willingness to think in new ways about their collections and their visions for their place in their world.

NOTES

1. "The Story of the World's First Public Museum," Ashmolean Museum, https://www.ashmolean.org/article/the-story-of-the-worlds-first-public-museum.
2. John E. Simmons, *Encyclopedia of Library and Information Sciences* (2010), s.v. "history of museums."
3. Kate Griffith, "The Blinding Whiteness of American Art Museums," Davidsonian, http://www.davidsonian.com/the-blinding-whiteness-of-american-art-museums/.
4. "Oakland Museum of California Cutting Staff, Restructuring," *Artforum*, April 5, 2021, https://www.artforum.com/news/oakland-museum-of-california-cutting-staff-re structuring-85429.
5. Alex Greenberger, "Baltimore Museum of Art Calls Off Controversial Deaccession Plan Hours before Sale," *ArtNews*, October 28, 2020, https://www.artnews.com/art-news/news/baltimore-museum-of-art-deaccession-called-off-sothebys-1234575295/.
6. Association of Art Museum Directors, "Art Museums by the Numbers 2015," https://aamd.org/sites/default/files/document/Art%20Museums%20By%20The%20Numbers%202015.pdf.
7. Kerr Houston, "How Mining the Museum Changed the Art World," *BmoreArt*, May 3, 2017, https://bmoreart.com/2017/05/how-mining-the-museum-changed-the-art-world.html.

14

What Makes a Museum a Museum

FROM THE AFRICAN EXPERIENCE

George Okello Abungu

INTRODUCTION

One of my most traumatizing moments in a long career with the museum world took place in the beautiful setting of Kyoto. It happened in a meeting space that has seen so many world achievements—including the Kyoto Protocol on climate change. In such a setting as the Kyoto International Conference Center, one would have expected that the museum world, through its umbrella organization of the International Council of Museums (ICOM), would reach another milestone—following in the footsteps of wise elders—by agreeing on the redefinition of the word "museum" through at least a compromise. This was not to be. The museum world left the symbolic venue at the end of the conference, not knowing what it stood for or what it was. Unfortunately, this also happened in a fast-changing world, and they deferred discussions and agreements, possibly hoping for some divine intervention.

With all kinds of excuses—ranging from uncertain government funding, inadequate participation in the definition process, and the language being too vague or too politically loaded—the museum community lost the opportunity to take charge of its destiny and, once and for all, engrain the museum position as critical and necessary in every country around the world. Instead, it became a laughingstock and platform for wrangling, and what happened after that does not require further elaboration. What was clear is that the museum world is still controlled and managed by White, conservative, elderly males.

The arrival of COVID-19 and, in the West, the Black Lives Matter movement caught museums totally unprepared. They could not demonstrate their critical relevance—especially in terms of the pandemic—leaving it to purely health and economic issues. Yet the pandemic is, first and foremost, a cultural and social issue. Most of the actions required, including social distancing, are cultural, which museums should have been natural, key players in advocating for through exhibitions and education programs that directly address those challenges.

Instead, they joined the rest of the chorus of victims, complaining about closures and job losses. They ceased to be critical institutions that could have worked with health services and politicians, among others, to deal with this issue and make their positions engrained in the annals of history. When the museum community failed to define itself at this crucial time, I realized that institutional decolonization and de-Europeanization were still pipe dreams. The Whiteness of museums was still intact, despite pronouncements to the contrary. But they have to decolonize for true change to occur.[1] It is now a bit late, and museums will have to work extra hard to regain the interest, trust, and confidence of communities, governments, the intellectual community, and all others who have a say in the heritage of humanity.

The stance of ICOM-US in Kyoto, in which it supported adopting the museum redefinition and, subsequently, discussion on this subject with a view to tackling the malaise, is not only a brave act but also a commendable initiative. History may be better at judging those who saw and recognized the future from the mountainside and wanted to move all the way to the top. The question "What makes a museum a museum?" came at the right moment.

This article is a critical analysis of the invaluable role museums could play for the needs of our present and future societies. The museum world is not only male-dominated; it is also White and conservative European. This must be addressed for any meaningful change to take place. It is not that museums can do or be everything to everybody. However, there is no reason why they cannot be something to everybody. Unfortunately, they are still caught up in the past. This is a past of Whiteness and male dominance, where change is a threat and must be avoided by all means possible.

MUSEUMS AS PEOPLE PLACES: THE HARD, UNCOMFORTABLE QUESTIONS

Although museums collect, care for, and exhibit material culture as well as other natural collections/specimens and works of art, among other objects, this is done for the benefit of people and society at large. It is people who give value to things considered part of our heritage. This is true for things that are tangible and intangible, movable and immovable, cultural and natural. However, museums also preserve our common heritage, where the past and present interact to ensure the future.

Museums, as a creation of the people, must, therefore, take care of the interest of society by promoting and protecting what has been given value as heritage. This must not, however, be done in such a way that heritage replaces people or that heritage or museum collections are protected for their own sake. It is more important that it is for the interest of humanity. Museums' relevance must be measured on their people-centeredness, where heritage becomes an added value to people's lives and their environment—rather than a thing unto its own.[2]

For this to happen, however, requires museums to deal with difficult, complex issues, some of which may not be seen as or considered traditional institutional responsibilities. This is even more true in times of challenge brought about by a pandemic, climate change, globalization, urbanization, and technological revolution. Population dynamics today—with those under forty (in the majority in many parts of the world) confronted with fewer jobs and opportunities but equally high expectations—call for all, including museums, to be adaptive to change.

Thus, museums can no longer be houses of curiosities, at best, for a privileged few at the taxpayers' expense. They must also be institutions that appeal to the underprivileged masses. They cannot only be the preserves of entitled curators, conservators, and researchers but for society as a whole.[3] Should this be the case, societal challenges must be at the core of protecting and promoting heritage and museum collections, including museum objects. These must, of necessity, also start to address societal challenges by taking advantage of rich museum resources.

Issues of a political nature, human rights, inclusion, gender, the needs of women and children, the discriminated, and the social and economic empowerment of communities must also fall under the museum agenda. This needs to happen in a way that dialogue on such matters is not shunned under the pretext that museums are apolitical, neutral spaces.[4] For what makes a museum a museum? Questions such as "How do we protect, promote, and use collections that speak to issues, engage communities in dialogue, and bring benefit to our lives?" are pertinent. Can we continue to ride on the premise that museums are "permanent institutions that exhibit, educate, and research both tangible and intangible heritage" (the current museum definition) without justifying how these collections positively impact human lives?

COVID-19 exposed museums through cuts in their budgets, loss of employment and positions, and lack of visitors, resulting in them not being considered crucial government concerns. Culture and the human behavior imprinted in many museum collections are critical to addressing the pandemic. Yet museums in general—and even those that consider themselves great institutions, with all their unique collections—were ineffective in demonstrating that. Instead of playing central roles, most museums became bystanders, watching from the periphery as they were emasculated. Museums could have been places of not only comfort and confidence building but also awareness creation and habit change. They could have operated as forums for discussion and dialogue and platforms for advocating the new normal.

Museums can no longer be silos incapable of defining their roles and what they are. The inability to immediately respond to a crisis such as the coronavirus pandemic and inaction during crucial moments, such as the demonstrated lukewarm response to Black Lives Matter, have exposed museums as noncritical institutions. This will continue as long as they disengage on matters concerning society and operate the way they have always done.

It is also clear that the language of today centers around sustainable development goals, climate change, and pandemics. However, how many museums can claim to speak to this? How many museums are involved in the discussion on climate change, human settlement, health, youth and unemployment, and conflict resolution? How many museums focus their exhibits on mechanisms of conflict resolution in the face of dwindling resources due to climate change, which threatens communal peace? How many effectively use their resources to create platforms for building peace? How many engage in dialogue, through exhibitions or public programs, on gender issues or job creation through cultural industries or other knowledge-based economies (of which museums have collections that speak to such creativity)? How many museums can claim to not only exhibit but also sustainably and positively use humanity's intangible heritage and knowledge systems for a better society?

These are the practices that hold and transmit traditions and create a common bond. The wisdom of the elders is held here to ensure harmony and equilibrium in societies, despite the diversity of humanity. The intangible power found in museum settings is through people and their actions, but museums are either incapable or unwilling to use this.

How many museums can pride themselves on engaging with communities in collaborative research, creation, exhibition, and curation? Are these not the minimum expectations of institutions in terms of their value and relevance to society today? Instead, museums are, in most cases, fixated on protecting and conserving objects—considered jewels in their collections—that are divorced from people, their needs, and the realities of today. Even the programs carried out in the name of education and public programs are hardly done in consultation with their communities and stakeholders. Museums globally are still held up by the belief that curators know it all and do it *for*, not *with*, their audiences.[5] It is a belief system that is fast running out of time and fashion, and if institutions do not change, they will soon become irrelevant and outdated.

THE DEBATE OF TODAY: WHAT NEXT?

For far too long, museums have operated under the pretext that they are critical. They hold heritage as crucial to national memory and identity. Some even branded themselves "universal,"[6] whereas others considered themselves "encyclopedic."[7] The mere existence of museums, in most cases, qualifies them for support (whether through public or private funding), and they have stayed in these comfort zones—avoiding difficult questions and discussions on matters that affect people and society in general. Some museums are considered to hold national assets, but what is their importance if they do not positively impact the lives of communities that pay for their upkeep and security? Why do they exist if they cannot engage in challenging, sometimes uncomfortable debates that help in the positive development of society?

Museums are not apolitical; they operate within the realms of politics.[8] Although they may not be platforms for politicking, they have to stand out, in many cases, as voices of reason in politically charged arenas. They cannot be quiet when people's lives are in danger because of what or who they are. This is what the Black Lives Matter movement taught us. They cannot be quiet when systems are looting and destroying heritage. We have heard voices of reason talk about conflicts in Iraq, Afghanistan, Syria, North Africa during the Arab Spring, and, later, the Sahel, along with many other places of warfare and heritage destruction. We see politically charged discussions on the issues of restitution currently bringing museums to the fore.[9] Therefore, they do not have the pleasure or privilege of hiding behind false notions of being apolitical and neutral.

In any case, these are not theoretical assumptions. A few museums globally have shown that they can make an impact beyond their traditional comfort zones. District Six Museum in Cape Town, founded during the inhumane rule of apartheid in South Africa, used memory and memorialization processes to resist the land appropriation of its communities. When South Africa achieved freedom in 1994, these memories were positively used to assist in the restoration of land rights to the rightful community holders. Here was the museum engaging on issues of human rights and addressing past injustices through memorialization.

Robben Island—a former jail notorious for detaining political dissenters during apartheid—became a museum to remind South Africa, and the world in general, that freedom is a human right. It is not easy to conquer the human spirit when there is a will to be free, and through narratives around the politics of oppression, the prison has become a symbol of remembrance and forgiveness. Museums can act as symbols of justice and just societies, for unjust memories are held within them. These memories should constantly remind us never to knowingly do wrong again. Although museums are not holy or sacred places, they can be witnesses to the injustices of the past and caution us against repeating them.

The Village Museum and House of Culture (part of the National Museum of Tanzania) has become one of the most active areas of performance regionally, including poetry reading and music, and promotes arts and artists—especially during this pandemic, when people in the arts are faced with severe challenges of survival. The museums here have moved away from the confinements of "dead objects" to create life and meaning in their pieces—they not only relate to communities, but also use the power of intangible heritage, such as poetry, performance, art, and music, to bring life and people into the museum.

The National Museums of Kenya (NMK) has been at the forefront of promoting Indigenous knowledge systems as well as using its heritage, especially around peace and conflict resolution, to assist communities in developing and maintaining harmony among themselves for years to come. This has been more in relation to pastoral societies, which compete for scarce resources, such as pasture and water for their animals, especially in times of unpredictable weather—possibly caused by climate change. These knowledge systems and practices have been documented further in books incorporating community voices.

The NMK has also been involved with communities in protecting and conserving constructed heritage and helping develop a knowledge base for conservation methods by training stonemasons and artisans in traditional building practices and craft making. Here is an institution that has broken imaginary permanent walls and created heritage spaces beyond the museum building.[10]

We live in a world where changes take place at supersonic speeds, where children born twenty years ago cannot understand the idea of phones as landlines with headsets, and where the concept of knowledge retention and transfer is of utmost importance. Museums could be involved in such exercises: going beyond the confines of their walls to work with communities in protecting, conserving, and promoting both the tangible and intangible. They also need to be proactive in wealth and job creation through knowledge retention, transfer, and sustainable use. Although not all institutions can be expected to do this, those that can, should be engaged, especially with programs that impact the well-being of the community.

On the island federation of St. Kitts and Nevis in the Caribbean, the Nevis Historical and Conservation Society serves as the custodian of Nevis's natural and cultural resources. The society runs three small museums and has been engaged with both natural (biodiversity) and cultural heritage protection beyond its walls since its inception in 1980. Since 2019, the Museum of Nevis History gift shop in Charlestown hosts a monthly "Meet the Artist" cocktail hour, where artists showcase and sell their work. Doing this not only preserves the heritage of the island but also helps to promote sustainable artistic creativity and contribute to the economy of the island. These examples demonstrate that museums can do more than just hold onto their collections, which, if not appropriately used, are of no relevance or value beyond being places of study for researchers and curators.

CONCLUSION

Times have changed, and museums have to change with the times. They cannot be averse to the critical issues of the moment. Although they may have great opportunities with new technologies, they also face grave competition from the

George Okello Abungu

same sector, especially in relation to audiences physically visiting the buildings. And although some remain a must-see with their collections of discovery and life-changing experiences, many may start to lose visitors as heritage is accessed through the internet. Soon, the majority of the population will be under thirty-five, born in the new millennium with huge technological innovations (and a love for them) and little attachment to physical museum collections, which will be seen as dead, redundant, and of the past.

Museums will either have to adapt technologically or consistently and carefully nurture younger audiences that are opinion makers who will promote the physical museum agenda—young researchers who are ready to dirty their hands behind the scenes and play advocacy roles for institutions. Otherwise, judging by the age of those attending the general ICOM conferences, museums will become a thing of the past, not the future. These are the people who have consistently refused change, and their continued presence and influence may soon render museums irrelevant, with, at best, museums about museums. Therefore, the future of institutions and their roles lies with the people, especially the youth and taxpayers, who vote in or out those who make laws, including those who decide on the financing of museums.

NOTES

1. See George Okello Abungu, "Museums: Geopolitics, Decolonization, Globalization and Migration," *Museum International* 71 (July 2019): 62–71; Raymond Silverman, George Okello Abungu, and Peter Probst, eds., *National Museums in Africa: Identity, History, and Politics* (New York: Routledge, 2022); and Shahid Vawda, "Museums and Epistemology of Injustice: From Colonialism to Decoloniality," *Museum International* 71 (July 2019): 72–79.
2. See George Okello Abungu, "Opening Up New Frontiers: Museum of the 21st Century," in *Museum 2000: Contribution or Challenge?*, eds. P. Agren and Sophie Nymen (Varnamo, Sweden: Fölth and Hössler, 2002), 37–43; George Okello Abungu, "Africa and Its Museums: Changing Pathways?," in *Art and Cultural Heritage: Law Policy and Practice*, ed. B. T. Hoffman (Cambridge: Cambridge University Press, 2009), 386–93; and Abungu, "Museums: Geopolitics, Decolonization, Globalization and Migration."
3. See Abungu, "Opening Up New Frontiers"; Abungu, "Africa and Its Museums"; Abungu, "Museums"; and E. N. Arinze, "African Museums: The Challenge of Change," *Museum International* 50, no. 1 (December 1998): 31–37.
4. See Abungu, "Museums."
5. See Abungu, "Museums."
6. See George Okello Abungu, "The Declaration: A Contested Issue," *ICOM News* 57, no. 1 (2004): 5; George Okello Abungu, "Universal Museums: New Contestations, New Controversies," in *UTI MUT: Past Heritage—Future Partnerships*, eds. M. Gabriel and J. Dahl (Copenhagen: IWGIA/NKA, 2008), 32–43; and Geoffrey Lewis, "The 'Universal Museum': A Case of Special Pleading?," in Hoffman, ed., *Art and Cultural Heritage*, 379–85.

7. See George Okello Abungu, "Encyclopedic Museums," in *Under Discussion: The Encyclopedic Museum*, ed. Donatien Grau (Los Angeles: Getty Research Institute, Getty Publications, 2021).

8. See Abungu, "Museums"; and Silverman, Abungu, and Probst, *National Museums in Africa*.

9. See George Okello Abungu, "The Question of Restitution and Return: A Dialogue of Interest in (Post) Colonialism and Cultural Heritage," *International Debates at the Humboldt Forum* (Berlin: Humboldt Forum, 2021); Dan Hicks, *The Brutish Museum: The Benin Bronzes, Colonial Violence and Cultural Restitution* (London: Pluto Press, 2020); Felwine Sarr and Benedicte Savoy, *The Restitution of African Cultural Heritage: Toward a New Relational Ethics* (Paris: French Ministry of Culture, 2018); and Silverman, Abungu, and Probst, *National Museums in Africa.*

10. See Abungu, "Opening Up New Frontiers"; and Abungu, "Africa and Its Museums."

15

The Work Is Never Done

RECKONING AND REPARATION IN MUSEUMS

Christopher Bedford

> The Baltimore Museum of Art embodies its commitment to artistic excellence, social equity, and local and global relevance in all of its work. From acquisitions to exhibitions and public programs, every Museum policy and practice, strategic decision, as well as the composition of the Board of Trustees, staff, and volunteers will be driven by these responsibilities.
>
> Bold, brave, and essential, it is the unwavering vision of The Baltimore Museum of Art to be the most relevant, publicly engaged museum in the United States and a dynamic model for all others.
>
> —Excerpt from the new Vision Statement of the Baltimore Museum of Art, adopted June 2018 by the board of trustees

Those statements capture what we live by in our work at the Baltimore Museum of Art (BMA) every day, across the whole of the museum hierarchy. We filter every decision we make at the institution through those values and principles, collaboratively and intentionally. And we understand ourselves—all of us—as forever a work in progress aimed toward a kind of restructuring that requires us to dismantle and reconstruct ourselves in a new and more effective form. We are abundantly aware at the BMA that we, like the vast, vast majority of institutions in this country, are historically White-centered. And, as such, we reflect a broader society that follows the same pattern. We are not an exception but, in fact, another symptom. And it is incumbent upon us to look at *all* of our systems of behavior in order to undo that center and create something quite different. This means that no aspect of our functioning should be exempt from scrutiny.

We discuss systemic change at the museum as broken down specifically into categories: exhibitions, acquisitions, public programs, staff, board, vendor decisions, and investment decisions. The list is probably incomplete, but you understand, I'm sure, the idea: all corners of the museum.

I was drawn to the opportunity to direct the BMA for a variety of reasons; obviously, the great existing collection, in combination with the board of trustees' vocal desire to radically change direction. I arrived in 2016 believing, as I do now, that we are living among a golden generation of Black American artists who are reconstructing wholly what it means to be an artist in society—not only producing the greatest and most relevant work in the world, but also prodding at the very definition of "artist." They are certainly adding to the formal lineages of abstraction and figuration and other modes of making, but also, and I think most critically, making different demands of themselves and museums to begin to service our publics differently—and, in fact, taking it further, to update our notion of publics.

I think it is interestingly serendipitous that a recent article appeared in the *New York Times* about the rise of Black abstraction and its new role in the market. The exhibition mentioned in that article was *Generations: A History of Black Abstract Art*, which was on view at the BMA from fall 2019 into the beginning of 2020. That show was the largest assembly of postwar abstraction produced by African American artists that any museum in this country has presented. And it was undertaken very deliberately in recognition of what had not been done historically in exhibition making and collection development. Concurrently, the contemporary collection galleries were reinstalled to highlight works by twentieth- and twenty-first-century African American artists. It was a sprint to catch up, an acknowledgment that a condition of equity can only be achieved through a period of reparation that recognizes, in turn and very straightforwardly, the bias of the past. The idea was then to further connect this grand and uncommon narrative with the experiences of a Black-majority city. And I think we were successful.

Following a similar principle of reckoning and reparation, in 2019, we analyzed the constitution of our collection as well as our exhibition history. We realized two things: first, our collection is 96 percent male—shocking, but not at all uncommon—and, second, we had never mounted a ticketed exhibition with a catalog focused on a woman artist in our more than hundred-year history. The year 2020 was the centennial of White women's suffrage in the United States, so, in acknowledgment of that long march toward universal suffrage, we decided to commit every exhibition, acquisition, and public program at the museum during that calendar year to the work of women artists—not because we were going to be able to substantively impact those percentages in our collection in one year, but to acknowledge, publicly, those biases and to announce the beginning of a long process of change aimed toward an eventual point of equity, one that I am sure will prove to be a forever receding finish line.

It probably goes without saying that reconstructing our collection is an enormous emphasis at the BMA. It is hardly a secret that in 2018, we sold seven paintings from our collection, all by White men. In the process, we managed to clear $18 million and have since been committing all of those funds to the acquisition of works by men and women of color for our postwar collection. When we took that action, it made waves in the museum world, but since then, esteemed museums such as the San Francisco Museum of Modern Art and the Art Gallery of Ontario in Toronto have followed suit, declaring their values and intent to change their collecting focus. And so, in 2021, the BMA mounted an exhibition, *Now Is the Time: Recent Acquisitions to the Contemporary Collection*, which presented, for the first time, many of the objects we brought into the collection with those proceeds and demonstrated the diverse, expansive stories we can now tell as a museum. That work begun in 2018 is ongoing.

To pivot to another part of our program, in 2019, we also established a satellite branch of the museum at Baltimore's Lexington Market, which is the longest continually operating public market in the United States. This is one of the initiatives of which I am most proud. By going to where people naturally gather with our program, rather than requiring that they come to us, we have been able to engage a wholly new audience through our work. This also is an ongoing effort, and an essential one in service to our community.

We have worked relentlessly to make sure there is symmetry between our city, who and what we say we are becoming, and who actually leads that charge, with the board of trustees being the highest form of governance at institutions such as the BMA. We have been successful to date in this effort, though, of course, we have a lot more work to do. In the interest of being self-critical, I think it is important to note that on July 1, 2022, Jim Thornton will take over as chair of our board, making him the first African American to lead our museum in 108 years. That is long overdue.

Staff leadership is, of course, equally important. We make diversity a priority in every hire, up to and including Dr. Asma Naeem, the Eddie C. and C. Sylvia Brown chief curator, who brings to her work an extraordinary background that weds a PhD in art history with a prior career of social justice work in the courtroom as a litigator. It remains my belief that the identity of a museum is rooted in its creative core. All emanates from there, and so it was imperative that we hire a person to lead that charge predisposed to lead with values. Asma is that person.

I want to close by gesturing toward what excites me most—namely, what is next. I think it has become a habit for institutions with an encyclopedic reach to rely on the postwar period to check diversity and equity boxes. The BMA has certainly been guilty of this, mounting in the past four years countless exhibitions of varying scales with a focus on the production of artists of color. We are, of course, very proud of this work and will continue to do it, but I think it represents an incomplete picture. For me, the most interesting and challenging task facing us in the next five years is to take our core values of diversity and equity and apply them to collecting and presenting works spanning all time and all geographies, across all of our collecting areas, and with all twenty-seven curators actively participating.

For instance, in December 2021, we dedicated two major new study centers at the museum. The first is the Ruth R. Marder Center for Matisse Studies, and the other is the Nancy Dorman and Stanley Mazaroff Center for the Study of Prints, Drawings, and Photographs (PDP). The PDP department at the museum accounts for roughly sixty-seven thousand of our total ninety-five thousand objects and is a collection capable of narrating a comprehensive history of Western art from the late fifteenth century to the present. The Matisse Center, on the other hand, is anchored by the largest holdings of Matisse's work in any public institution in the world. Both centers are vital to the continued growth and development of the museum, and, critically, both will participate in diversifying and complicating the art history we present to our audiences. What the curators in charge of those centers conjure to advance our broader vision is extraordinarily exciting to me.

The need for structural change in art museums is deep and long-standing. Although this essay is a brief and necessarily incomplete overview, I hope it gives a keen sense of the Baltimore Museum of Art's work, our convictions, and our commitment to a systemic approach as the best route to sustainable institutional change.

Christopher Bedford

16

"Dysmantaling" a Museum

Christina Woods

There is no better place to work than a museum or art institute. There is no better place to research than in a museum or an art institute. There is no better place to broaden your world than in a museum or art institute. So what happens when that museum or art institute has only a single story, a portion of a story, or worse yet, a story of supremacy?

Boozhoo gakina awiya. Makwa indoodem. Anamacikwe indigoo. Mesaabekong indoonjibaa.[1]

This is a classic Anishinaabe greeting. It reads: "Hello all. My clan is the bear. My name is Thunderbird Lady. I live in Duluth, Minnesota." Mesaabekong is on one of the world's largest bodies of freshwater. It has been a confluence of culture since long before European history began here. Mesaabekong was a trading port for goods and medicine and a thoroughfare connecting communities from the Arctic Circle to the salt waters of the south. I share this greeting to demonstrate how most reading this essay have not heard or seen this Indigenous language of the United States.

You may also not know the cultural identity of the Anishinaabe, and as you learn about the Indigenous group, it will be through a colonized lens. The interpretations and teaching will be skewed toward the White dominant culture to develop understanding. This is due to the history of my ancestors not being included in the historical accounts of the United States. You see, in the United States, a practice began when Europeans colonized this land: a system was established to benefit a specific race of people, Whites. Over hundreds of years of European immigration to the United States, fleeing persecution in their homelands, they set up systems to benefit themselves at the expense of the Indigenous peoples who were already here. These systems were essentially coping strategies to help Whites dismantle their trauma. Why? And what does this have to do with museums of the future?

Well, the "why" is to support the creation of a "more perfect union" that addresses this trauma that Europeans were carrying. This is the single story the United States was built upon. To create a more perfect union, control of the resources, the government, and the "Indian" was imperative. One way this control was established was by creating a more positive narrative about Whites and a savage, beastlike, and inhumane narrative about the "Indian." This binary lens still exists today inside art institutes and museums, driving a single story, a portion of the story, and the imbalance of White as the dominant culture.

What does this have to do with museums? Museums and art institutes are principal drivers of documenting and perpetuating historical narratives that demonstrate dominant cultural ideals. Museums and art institutes propel awareness about the power of implicit bias to create culture while silencing and making invisible cultural aspects that do not support assimilation into the dominant culture. Below, I share three imperative actions that will create a more inclusive museum and art experience of the future.

UNDERSTAND INSTITUTIONAL HISTORY

The first action is to understand institutional history. This awakening must include how the land under the bricks and mortar of the institution was obtained, the history of exhibitions and the narratives they have supported and left out, and the history of how funding has acted as the gatekeeper of art collected and shown. I like to think of this step as an exercise in seeking the true name of the institute for its actual work, such as the Institute of White Men's Art or the Museum of Unnatural History. When coupled with a time line, this exercise establishes the single story of the institute. Seeking the truth of an organization and the truth of wealth's influence on collections and museums and its impact on underrepresented communities is imperative. Institutions must deaccession pieces in collections to dismantle harmful narratives and make space for underrepresented stories.

The organization I serve, the Duluth Art Institute, began with a mission 113 years ago that was "art for all." The founders showed art in city jails, the city hall, and various other pop-up venues. But the art displayed was mostly created by well-established, White, male artists. Over time, and most recently, exhibitions at the Duluth Art Institute became more inclusive, but the didactics remained White-centric, so the evolution of didactic writing to erase the White lens through which we talk about art was started. We then looked closely at how shows were selected and reduced bias by enlisting a diverse community panel to select all the exhibitions for the institute. Within our own collections, we diversify the narratives and include the voice of the underrepresented community in the didactics, including the issues with any dominant narrative that drove a negative story or erased history to benefit Whiteness.

ENGAGE UNDERREPRESENTED PEOPLE

The second action is a robust effort to survey and engage underrepresented people. This involves not only hiring people who carry this burden of underrepresentation, but also using input from the often smaller groups of people who are negatively impacted by the museum or institute. The status quo of museums and institutes is supported by the White experience, either because it represents the most common denominator or because of the single story bias. When weight is placed on survey responses that reveal absent narratives rather than the dominant experience, museums and art institutes can dismantle and rebuild with a commitment to challenge deeply rooted biases. Museums and institutes need to engage a community panel of diverse individuals representing race, cultural identity, gender, LGBTQ+ (lesbian, gay, bi, trans, queer, questioning), ability, and socioeconomic experiences. The community panel must have a strong say in selecting and examining incoming exhibitions and work closely with the curator to design opportunities to divulge the truth about the works. This, in turn, leads to developing a diverse board of directors, trustees, and donors as essential elements in dismantling colonization.

At the Duluth Art Institute, we have a 113-year history as a predominantly White organization. In 2020, we weighted the insight and experiences of BIPOC (Black, Indigenous, people of color) artists: 2 percent of our entire constituency of artists. These insights drive the changes to create a BIPOC-led arts organization. We had to address Whiteness as a power dynamic and adjust to create a more inclusive experience for all. Because we're so used to the colonialized power dynamic of Whiteness, we don't notice where it shows up. It becomes implicit, unconscious, invisible, and we get comfortable with it, even among BIPOC, as a result of assimilation into Whiteness. People seek comfort by fitting in. We needed to bring in diverse perspectives, not only to broaden our view, but also to provide support for the less familiar experiences. BIPOC leadership made an enormous difference in how we approach our mission, select art exhibitions, and develop educational programming. I challenge museums and art institutes to dismantle their colonized standard of operations.

ACCESS FOR ALL

Third, all art institutes and museums must open access to all. What does this look like? Each organization must delve into its history and context. The hardest part is determining how to include people who have been traditionally excluded. Much of that work depends on the dismantling of personal, professional, and cultural biases, both implicit and overt. I hope that today you're able to open yourselves up to understanding the ideologies around colonialism and the supremacy of Whiteness as a culture and the power in both. White ideals such as perfection, having to be an expert, and infallibility perpetuate supremacy. These are organizational ideals and characteristics that drive how we are included or fit in.

The work that we've been doing at the Duluth Art Institute is much broader than the Anishinaabe homelands where I live. This lens lends itself to being inclusive of diverse, absent narratives. The first step we took to dismantle and rebuild the organization was decolonizing. We needed to be honest about the fact that museums were funded, opened, and supported by Whiteness. And when I speak of Whiteness, it is the *ideology* of Whiteness that pushes a single story. I hope that you're able to open yourselves up to understanding the ideologies around colonialism, even being supreme (that is, ideal and normative) as a White person, which is white supremacy. I hope you can open yourselves up to looking at your organizations and, most important, yourself and thinking about how that negatively impacts people and communities by leaving out narratives.

The work of dismantling involves decolonization, and that needs to be addressed on all levels: the board of directors, leadership, collections, exhibitions and didactics, funders, and operational policies. It is imperative to understand what it takes to make space for all things beyond Whiteness. Other areas of operation that were tackled and continue to evolve are the policies and team guide. A good look revealed Whiteness as the standard in holidays, sick leave, and even what professionalism looks like. There was a need to dismantle the ideal of what an arts leader must be in order to fulfill the position professionally. Is an arts degree necessary to have a vision or something to say about the narratives held in place?

Artists, too, play a part in supporting a single story. Arts organizations must understand the movement among artists and leaders in Indigenous communities to know what is acceptable. Institutes must recognize the Indian Arts and Crafts Act and hold artists to this standard. In my region, it is unacceptable for a White person to create work that depicts Indigenous people in regalia or their faces without permission. In other words, if you are a painter, you cannot use a photo taken of Indigenous people to paint from. This is very important. Indigenous people have been subjected to Whites portraying them as part of a landscape for too long.

White artists have also abused the sacredness and artistic nature of regalia through their belief that they are entitled to photograph, paint, and replicate works of art on dolls and in the fashion industry, for example. Art institutes and museums still display and own this type of art because it was created by famous people and supports an unconscious bias about how representation of the "Indian" looks. There is a movement in Indian Country to dismantle this practice, but it is not restricted to Indigenous people—this standard applies to all underrepresented cultures and people. Cultural narratives, especially, must be told by individuals within that culture, which means the individuals are involved and have control over the image, didactics, and use. This also means they get paid.

On the financial side, funders need to be accountable as well. To the victor goes the spoils, but the victor also gets to write the history and often funds the museum that houses the history. This locks in a story built on the unearned credibility of the victor and the victor's wealth. The wealth of many institutions and funders is built on the backs of stolen land and slavery. And it's time to recognize it. And it's time for reparations around it. Funders must research the generation of wealth that funds museums and institutions. It behooves funders to require a standard of practice that demonstrates truth and reconciliation among museums and institutes. That truth and reconciliation must include a standard that supports paid and dedicated board seats for underrepresented people and a commitment to operational policies and practices that support underrepresented individuals in leadership positions.

DYSMANTALISM

This is a systemic change. To build museums and institutes of the future, the time is now. We are on the cusp of a new art era, an era of artists, museums, institutes, patrons, and funders moving into what I'm calling Dysmantalism. Yes, with a "y," because if change doesn't happen, we risk going deeper into dystopia.

As an Anishinaabe Indigenous woman in this nation, in this country of the United States, I grapple every day with overt, negative impacts on Indigenous nations by systems that support Whiteness as the norm. Art institutes and museums, in an ideal future, will be places where all people can learn how to dismantle their biases and understanding of the world. With this, I propose that all art institutes and museums embark on Dysmantalism.

This is the opportunity to disrupt centuries of learning that determined who mattered. If leaders in the arts don't drive a new narrative, we will have to add to the already broken narratives a new one: the support of dystopia for already stressed populations. Dysmantalism has started to break open wounds in order to build something better. Dysmantalism is, I believe, a movement of artists and institutions working together to make space for underrepresented narratives, truth, and reconciliation that will challenge the status quo and push open the tight boundaries designed to represent Whiteness.

Institutional leaders need thoughtful reflection before diving into acts of dismantling. Predominantly White organizations need to prepare for the discomfort of real change. This form of dismantling is rough. It's hard work. It involves working on yourself as an individual assimilated into Whiteness and understanding your role in being an assimilator. It can feel very, very personal and threatening, as much of what was relayed culturally will be filtered into incongruent pieces of untruths.

It's imperative that organizations don't rush into this and practice thoughtful reflection around what is missing internally to help all people in the organization be successful. So many organizations, including those outside the arts sector, are implicitly based on Whiteness and implicitly support long-held and deeply rooted ideas that promote Whiteness and leave out everything else. I challenge everyone to do the work of identifying who you are in Whiteness and what single story you rely on. If 2020 has taught us anything, it is the importance of dismantling business as usual in order to be willing to face significant change. If you don't dismantle bias, you have absent narratives that are the pain points in your organization.

My work at the intersection of visual art and diversity, equity, and inclusion is to recognize complacency in Whiteness. Museums and institutes of the future could be places where people can dismantle biases, model equity and inclusion, and hold us to a standard of respecting human dignity. Dysmantalism is how we will disrupt the single story, a partial story, and the practice of White supremacy in museums and art institutes.

NOTE

1. *Miigwech* to *Naawakwe* Bill Howes, for assisting with the spelling of the Anishinaabemowin used in this chapter.

Part Five
Museums as Influencers

17

The Museum with the Community

Diana Pardue

Museums have a shared commitment, responsibility, and authority in relationship to their communities. Museums are places of learning and exploration, key institutions for influence and dissemination of public scholarship. What does it mean for museums to be influencers in their communities? How can museums best portray the identity and memory of their communities? How can museums not only chronicle the past but also depict the present and become touchstones for the future of their communities? Three distinguished essayists, Kelly McKinley, Lauran Bonilla-Merchav, and Lisa Sasaki, discuss these questions in the enlightening essays that follow this overview.

McKinley's essay explores the question of what makes a museum a museum by using the informative case study of her own experience of implementing programming changes at the Oakland Museum of California and then taking a step back to analyze and document the institution's specific influence on its local community.

Bonilla-Merchav's essay connects directly to the issue of the new definition of "museum," pointing out that the definition is important, not only within the statutes of ICOM, but as a reference point for countless arts and culture organizations. The new definition will ultimately serve as a benchmark for museums and museum professionals globally from which to derive their own methods of community influence. According to Bonilla-Merchav and Bruno Soares, "while there are still some museum professionals that do not wish to see a change, the incisive work of the MDPP, which substantially recommended a revision, and the majority of authors who have published on the matter, imply that the sector is ripe for a new definition."

Sasaki's essay responds to the challenge of creating meaningful influence by prioritizing people, embracing a community service mentality, questioning their missions and institutional practices and histories, and ultimately pushing beyond the comfort zone to truly become agents of change.

To summarize the engaging discussions of these three notable essayists, museums can be influencers only if they truly see and understand the people whom they serve. Museums are about people, not just things—they are institutions of community connectivity and social service. Stephen E. Weil, the distinguished and renowned leader in the United States museum community, was known for stating that museums need to transform from being "about something" to being "for somebody."[1] This brief characterization of what a museum can be is packed with information about what a museum does and whom it serves. And it aligns very much with the earlier discussion in Part Two: "Safe Places or Social Spaces?" Should museums be satisfied with the roles they have traditionally held, or is it time to question and perhaps expand their role? If museums do not evolve, do not change, do they get left behind?

And so, from Weil's quote comes the notion, further discussed in the following essays, that museums are about people, not just things. And museums can be very important as influencers or institutions of community connectivity and social service. Sasaki's answer to people's adverse reaction on the concept of museums prioritizing community involvement is, "Why not?" Understanding, of course, that museums do not necessarily have the infrastructure or knowledge to distribute public services in the same manner as organizations where that is their primary function, museums have no reason not to embrace a service mentality.

The final point, which has generated a fair amount of discussion, is that museums should be open to all perspectives, as they are a gathering place, a civic and social space. They need to make room for multiple voices and make more space at the table. The question is: Are museums a place or space with or without a viewpoint in service of dynamic public impact and permanent societal contributions? Are they just a gathering place for chatting and conversation? Or is the museum a place where decisions need to be made about which parts of the conversation should be carried forward by the museum itself for external impact? The answer, especially in the context of what the world has gone through in 2020–2021, is of great significance for the future of museums. Museums in the twenty-first century are in a state of transformation. As McKinley states in her essay, "defining the museum with people as central to its purpose and social outcomes as its measure of impact and value is imperative for the long-term sustainability and relevance of these organizations."

As we emerge from a global pandemic, the need and opportunity for museums to serve and communicate to communities and define their value to society in a different, more relevant way has never been more important. The twenty-first century promises to be very interesting from the standpoint of museum practice.

NOTE

1. Stephen E. Weil, "From Being *about* Something to Being *for* Somebody: The Ongoing Transformation of the American Museum," in "American Museums," *Daedalus: Journal of the American Academy of Arts and Sciences* 128, no. 3 (1999): 229–58.

18

To Be of Influence Starts with Being Open to Influence

Kelly McKinley

"How are we a museum?," a trustee asked me at the end of my first board of directors meeting—a surprising yet perfectly reasonable question, I suppose, given long-standing definitions of museums as places that collect, study, and exhibit the artifacts and phenomena of our human and natural histories.

So, what does make a children's museum a museum? My response to the trustee was that the Bay Area Discovery Museum is a museum like any other by its definition: a place where people come together to understand the world and their place in it. Some museums do that through art, others through natural science specimens, and children's museums such as ours do it through immersive, play-based, hands-on experiences. Although this is not a broadly shared definition of a museum, it signals how I believe we need to evolve the definition from a description of what we do to the impact we wish to have in people's lives. Defining the museum with people as central to its purpose and social outcomes as its measure of impact and value is imperative for the long-term sustainability and relevance of these organizations. Evolving the definition to focus on social impact will also require new structures, roles, skills, and tasks for the people who work in and govern museums.

The great American museum scholar Stephen E. Weil, in a 1999 article for *Daedalus*, characterized the ongoing and increasingly urgent transformation of museums in the United States as being from "about something to for somebody."[1] This phrase is credited to Michael Spock and his team at the Boston Children's Museum in 1961 in Joanne Cleaver's 1992 survey of children's museums. Weil described the history of American museums as starting with the warehouse and salvage business, evolving into the "refreshment" or entertainment business, and now needing to embrace public service.[2] Twenty-two years later, as the world emerges from a global pandemic and communities across the United States demand racial and social justice and equity, the urgency and opportunity for museums to serve communities and their needs and desires have never been greater.

When they define themselves and their purpose in terms of how they make a difference in people's lives, museums have the potential to create positive social change in their communities. Starting with the most pressing needs and interests of their community and imagining how a museum's assets and expertise might uniquely be brought to bear on solutions and opportunities will position museums as part of essential community infrastructure, part of an ecosystem of organizations that serve the well-being of the whole community.

For museums to influence social change, they will need new ways of working and, ultimately, new kinds of relationships, with communities. Influence is predicated on trust—a relationship created and sustained through dialogue, reciprocity, inclusion, and openness. The colonial foundations and racist and classist histories of museums in the United States mean that many communities, in particular low-income communities and communities of color, do not feel seen or served by cultural institutions. To be beloved and of use to the whole community will take more than a just a shift in how we define our purpose and impact. It will take a flip or an upending of the traditional museum paradigm.

Some examples of the paradigm shift required to center social impact include moving from:

Inside Out to Outside In—museums starting with what's happening in their community, rather than with their collections, when developing programming and resources. The collections still play a central role, but they become a means to an end as opposed to an end in and of themselves.

Transactional to Relational—museums defining their value and purpose in terms of the relationships they build and nurture with communities, and the outcomes they hope to see in people's lives over time, rather than the exhibits and programs they deliver.

Collections to Capital—museums thinking about their assets and resources in more expansive ways, beyond collections and scholarship and real estate to human, social, and financial capital, and how all those resources can be deployed in service of community needs and interests.

Consumption to Cocreation—museums embracing the principle of "nothing about us without us is for us" and working with community to identify and tell the stories that are relevant and resonant to people's lives. This also involves museums moving away from speaking with a single expert voice and creating a platform for many different voices and ways of knowing, making room for lived experience alongside scholarly knowledge.

Container to Convener—museums thinking about themselves less as repositories and presenters of collections, and more as conveners of people with the collections and exhibits serving as the brokers of curiosity, conversation, connection, and, ultimately, the creation of meaning and understanding.

What might this shift, or flip, look like in practice, in a museum trying to exercise its power and influence in more community- or people-centered ways? I will share the example of one organization, the Oakland Museum of California (OMCA), where I served as deputy director from 2014 to 2019. OMCA is a museum of art, history, and natural science located in the heart of downtown Oakland, founded in 1969 as "the museum of the people." Over the past dozen years or so, prior to the pandemic, building on four decades of community-engaged, local issues-based exhibition development and programming, the museum had essentially doubled its audience and was attracting a significantly more diverse audience, with more than 50 percent identifying as people of color and the majority under the age of forty-five, including many families with children.

OMCA had been consciously evolving its practice and thinking over many years to embrace its democratic founding mission. In 2010 it undertook a major project to reimagine and reinstall all ninety thousand square feet of its permanent collection galleries in art, science, and natural history. Community consultation and collaboration informed every aspect of the project, including which stories were told, which objects were shown, and how the experiences were designed to maximize interaction and learning for people of all ages and backgrounds.[3]

In 2013, the museum launched Friday Nights@OMCA, a free weekly all-ages evening event that featured food trucks, live music, dancing, and programming across the campus and galleries. These two projects played a significant role in transforming who came to the museum. But what did these dramatic shifts in attendance and visitor demographics really mean? What were the implications and potential of the museum now that it was serving a broader and more diverse audience? Museum staff started seeking a way to both articulate and measure how the museum was making a difference in people's lives and in the larger community. We then set about determining our theory of change— the "so what," or impact, of all our work for the people we served. As a first step, we asked ourselves to identify which problems or challenges people in Oakland were facing that we as a museum might be uniquely equipped to help solve.

Oakland was undergoing significant fallout from generations of inequities within institutions, the state, and civil society resulting in a decline in social cohesion and an increase in social exclusion. Schools and neighborhoods were increasingly segregated, the income divide was more pronounced, and the erosion of public space and safety meant that people had few places where they could convene and interact with those from different neighborhoods, people different from themselves. We landed on social fragmentation as a pressing community issue that we felt both equipped and inspired to begin helping to solve. Expressed otherwise, OMCA identified social cohesion as a community outcome it would attempt to influence.[4]

With greater social cohesion as OMCA's theory of change, all activities from collecting to exhibitions and public programming prioritized creating the space and context for greater connection, trust, and understanding among individuals and social groups. We developed four indicators that would tell us we were achieving that impact. Those indicators were that visitors would tell us

1. I felt welcome here,
2. I saw my stories and identities reflected here,
3. I had the opportunity to connect with other people, and
4. I had an opportunity to express my point of view and consider those of others.

These indicators focused on welcome, inclusion, social interaction, and openness to diverse perspectives—all sociocultural requisites for the creation of trust, human connection, and social cohesion.

OMCA's 2016 exhibition *All Power to the People: Black Panthers at 50* is a case study that illustrates what can happen when museums flip the paradigm and center community needs, interests, and perspectives; cocreate experiences; and focus on social impact. Working in partnership with members of the Black Panther Party and local Black activists, the exhibition told stories of the party's work and impact that didn't make the news and the legacy of that work today. These stories included the party's work in education, senior care, and food security, and the powerful role women played in its social service origins. This exhibition attracted more visitors than any special exhibition in the museum's history. Evaluators observed and documented visitors of all ages actively engaged with the exhibit and each other. During exit interviews, many visitors noted that their perspectives about the Black Panthers were changed. Visitors also shared that they believed the museum was telling important Oakland stories, creating a platform for histories that museums often shied away from for fear of controversy, and bringing people together to foster understanding.[5]

By prioritizing these sociocultural indicators across all our work, and surveying for them weekly and year-round, we inferred that over time we would be creating greater social cohesion. These indicators shaped how we described and measured our impact, guided how we designed our experiences and programs, and defined how we hoped to hold ourselves accountable to each other, our stakeholders, and the community we served.[6] By describing and measuring the role and impact in terms of community service—serving people and to what end—we were able to transform how people in Oakland understood the value of the museum, how they engaged with the museum, and the kinds of people who invested in the museum.[7]

In 1971, at its ninth General Conference, the International Committee on Museums (ICOM) membership adopted a resolution rejecting the traditional concept of a museum with its emphasis on collecting and collections. The resolution urged a complete reassessment of their publics' needs so that museums might define their purpose in relation to their social context and "more firmly establish their educational and cultural role in the service of mankind."[8] In 1984, the American Association (now Alliance) of Museums (AAM) published *Museums for a New Century*, the report of a commission established to study and clarify the role of museums in American society. Among the commission's recommendations was the need for museums to embrace their educational role more fully, to describe more adequately the contributions they make to the quality of human experience, and to ensure that their staff and boards more fully reflect the diversity of the communities they seek to serve.[9] Eight years later, as an outgrowth of *Museums for a New Century* and against a backdrop of global change, AAM published *Excellence and Equity: Education and the Public Dimension of Museums*. The report called for a fundamental change in how museums view their service to society and argued that "museums perform their most fruitful public service by providing an educational experience in the broadest sense: by fostering the ability to live productively in a pluralistic society and to contribute to the resolution of the challenges we face as global citizens."[10]

Given more than fifty years of leadership and advocacy for a new definition and role for museums, why has the field been so slow to change? Why do museums continue to define their purpose and value so narrowly in terms of their activities and outputs? Part of the answer lies in museum power dynamics and hierarchy, with curatorial and collections departments traditionally holding most of the decision-making power, and most museum directors rising out of curatorial ranks. For museums to fulfill their potential as social influencers, space needs to be made for new kinds of skills and new ways of working, with authority shared across content and engagement teams internally, and externally with communities and other stakeholders. Another part of the answer lies in the belief that when a museum becomes less of a cause and more of an instrument for social good, then the so-called quality of scholarship, display, and interpretation is eroded and the organization's stature and authority are diminished. Many museums exist across the country and the world where these ideas and commitments are not mutually exclusive, and the organizations have earned a more prominent and essential role in the social infrastructure and lives of their communities.

The future sustainability of museums rests on making a different kind of case for their role and purpose in society—a purpose to serve people, their needs and dreams. It means thinking about not just how the collections but all the museum's assets and resources are brought to bear on the challenges facing the people they serve. By shifting from *about* something to *for* somebody, by being open and responsive to the social conditions in which they find themselves, museums can become beloved, inclusive, and useful institutions with the power to influence real social change.

NOTES

1. Stephen E. Weil, "From Being *about* Something to Being *for* Somebody: The Ongoing Transformation of the American Museum," in "American Museums," *Daedalus: Journal of the American Academy of Arts and Sciences* 128, no. 3 (1999): 229–58.
2. Joanne Cleaver, *Doing Children's Museums* (Charlotte, VT: Williamson Publishing, 1992), 9.
3. The community-engaged reinstallation of the permanent collection art galleries is documented in Barbara Henry and Kathleen McLean, eds., *How Visitors Change Our Museum: Transforming the Gallery of California Arts at the Oakland Museum of California* (Oakland: Oakland Museum of California, September 2010).
4. Kelly McKinley, "What Is Our Museum's Social Impact," *Medium*, July 10, 2017, https://medium.com/new-faces-new-spaces/what-is-our-museums-social-impact-62525fe88d16.
5. Johanna Jones, "What Problem in Our Community Is Our Museum Uniquely Equipped to Solve?" *Medium*, January 23, 2019, https://medium.com/new-faces-new-spaces/what-problem-in-our-community-is-our-museum-most-uniquely-equipped-to-solve-fe4dce9848b7.
6. Johanna Jones, "Quantifying Our Museum's Social Impact," *Medium*, May 14, 2020, https://medium.com/new-faces-new-spaces/quantifying-our-museums-social-impact-e99bff3ef30e.
7. Lori Fogarty, "How Defining and Measuring Social Impact Changed Our Museum," *Medium*, May 14, 2020, https://medium.com/new-faces-new-spaces/how-defining-and-measuring-social-impact-changed-our-museum-9b9c2305852c.
8. *ICOM News 71* (September 1971): 47.
9. *Museums for a New Century: A Report of the Commission on Museums for a New Century* (Washington, DC: American Association of Museums, 1984).
10. *Excellence and Equity: Education and the Public Dimension of Museums* (Washington, DC: American Association of Museums, 1992), 7.

19

Can a New Definition Convert Museums into Influencers?

Lauran Bonilla-Merchav and Bruno Brulon Soares

In this section, both Lisa Sasaki and Kelly McKinley argue that yes, in fact museums can be influencers, particularly within their own communities. They can steer their public's awareness in a direction that may lead toward a more sustainable future, while strengthening the historic bonds and present relationships that hold fast their communities. Many museums today feel this is the path they must follow to remain relevant in society, and they are charting their course on such principles. International Council of Museums (ICOM)'s current museum definition, nonetheless, does not require this of museums, and as a new definition proposal is in the process of being crafted, it is interesting to consider whether the museum definition will convert museums into influencers. By this is meant that a new definition perhaps may lead museums to serve as entities that positively impact society, beyond their role in heritage preservation and communication, benefiting communal and environmental harmony.

This conception of the museum's social role, present since the 1972 Round Table in Santiago, Chile, has been ratified by 195 countries that adopted the 2015 UNESCO "Recommendation Concerning the Protection and Promotion of Museums and Collections, Their Diversity and Their Role in Society," drafted with ICOM support. The recommendation considers "museums as spaces for cultural transmission, intercultural dialogue, learning, discussion and training, [that] also play an important role in education (formal, informal, and lifelong learning), social cohesion and sustainable development."[1]

It is impossible to know at present how many museums abide by what UNESCO calls upon them to do, to directly influence society beyond their particular confines. But it is certain that many museums do not heed the call to be socially responsible. Throughout its history in the twentieth and twenty-first centuries, ICOM aligned its global actions and influence with those of UNESCO and other transnational organizations, aiming to persuade museums around the world of their active social role. Created in a post–Second World War, European context, ICOM has been responsible for fostering museums that work closely with societies, proposing a common agenda based on notions such as "local development," "community participation," "democracy," and environmental preservation.[2]

More recently, in 2019, ICOM adopted the resolution "on sustainability and the adoption of Agenda 2030, Transforming Our World," recognizing "that all museums have a role to play in shaping and creating a sustainable future"; endorsing the call "for museums to respond through rethinking and recasting their values, missions, and strategies"; recommending that museums "become familiar with, and assist in all ways possible, the goals and targets of the UN SDGs"; and suggesting that museums be empowered by Agenda 2030, "acknowledging and reducing our environmental impact, including our carbon footprint, and helping secure a sustainable future for all inhabitants of the planet: human and non-human."[3] In so doing, the organization set principles that further guide museum work, linking directly to the urgency of Agenda 2030.

The museum profession is most definitely evolving, but perhaps too slowly. The contentious shift is reflected in the ongoing debate around ICOM's museum definition, which many feel does not address the above-mentioned calls to action. Since 2015, ICOM has been engaged in a revision of its current definition: "A museum is a non-profit, permanent institution in the service of society and its development, open to the public, which acquires, conserves, researches, communicates and exhibits the tangible and intangible heritage of humanity and its environment for the purposes of education, study and enjoyment." This widely cited definition, nearly intact since the 1970s, reflects the perspective set forth by a few representatives of the museum sector. When approved in 1974, a maximum of fifteen professionals per country could be active members. Nonetheless, a statute change that same year put ICOM on the verge of becoming a more democratic and populous global forum, today counting more than forty thousand members from 141 countries.[4]

The definition, amended in 2007, remains attached to this part of ICOM history, but in the following decade a discussion for its full revision began, in an aim to more broadly represent actual museum practice and further enable diverse social groups to claim their right to memory and the preservation of their cultural heritage. A working group was formed in 2015, and later ICOM's executive board (EB) named the Museum Definition, Prospects and Potentials

(MDPP) Standing Committee, presided over by Jette Sandahl, in January 2017. As Sandahl writes, MDPP

> systematically explored, researched and observed current societal trends as they impact museums, and analysed the historic background and the epistemological roots of the museum concept. It has listened to museum communities and discussed with them the shifts in paradigms that have appeared, unevenly and incompletely, but still consistently, in the relationship between museums and the societies around us.[5]

The MDPP conducted work for nearly two years, first assessing whether the museum definition needed to be revised and then recommending a revision and submitting five proposals to the EB for their selection of one to be voted on at the extraordinary general assembly in Kyoto in 2019.[6] The selected proposal (edited by the EB to stipulate that museums must be nonprofit)[7] unleashed a heated debate before, during, and after the Kyoto conference. Ultimately, a vote on a new museum definition was postponed, and the dispute was succinctly summarized by the *New York Times* (words in brackets added to better reflect the issue at hand):

> For some, these disagreements reflect a wider split in the museum world about whether such institutions should be places that exhibit and research artifacts [only], or ones that actively engage with political and social issues [as well].[8]

It is obviously not as simple as this, and the benefits and problems in the current definition and the 2019 proposal have been argued by many authors in a vast array of publications and podcasts that have emerged on the topic (*Museum International*, ICOFOM, AAM, *Curator: The Museum Journal*, among many others). Although some museum professionals still do not wish to see a change, the incisive work of the MDPP, which substantially recommended a revision, and the majority of authors who have published on the matter, imply that the sector is ripe for a new definition.[9]

Regarding the current definition, authors have tackled the inappropriateness of terms such as "permanent institution" or "enjoyment." But for some professionals and ICOM members, what seems most deficient is the lack of a direct call to museums to be the kind of influencers discussed in this section. Little emphasis is on the social responsibility of museums, summarized by the "5 Ps" of the UN's Sustainable Development Goals: people, planet, prosperity, peace, and partnerships. The current use of "in the service of society and its development" can be seen as vague, and some museum professionals want a definition that addresses more specifically the primary concerns with which museums should contend in a world living with crisis. Yet others decry that museums are dedicated to heritage preservation and that they are unqualified to address wider social problems, despite the UNESCO recommendation and the 2019 ICOM resolution.

So, what are the majority of museums professionals around the world willing to take on as part of their commitment to humanity? This is what the methodology created by the new Standing Committee for the Museum Definition, ICOM Define (established in December 2020), is aiming to find out in the process of arriving at a museum definition proposal to be voted on at ICOM's general conference in Prague in August 2022.

When the vote on a new definition was postponed in 2019, one aspect clear to both of us now cochairing ICOM Define was the need that committees expressed for greater consultation on the matter. There seemed a general satisfaction with the direction taken by MDPP; but the body of ICOM representatives made evident that they wanted to be taken into account if a new definition was to be adopted. Throughout ICOM's history, the museum definition has been altered on seven occasions.[10]

But the 2019 proposal was a complete break with the past, generating concern and upset in many constituents. Therefore, considering the need to more widely survey ICOM committees, the methodology designed by five members of ICOM Define—Chedlia Annabi (Tunisia), Inkyung Chang (South Korea), Nava Kessler (Israel), Diana Pardue (United States), Juliette Raoul-Duval (France), and the two of us—incorporates four rounds of consultation with ICOM committees (national, international, regional alliances, and affiliated organizations). Thus, the consultation process is based on the structure of ICOM's advisory council, enabling each committee to take part in the process by responding to surveys sent out and widely publicized. In structuring the consultations by committees, members had the opportunity to share their perspective twice, considering that every member is affiliated with a national committee and can be active in one international committee.

As we write this in October 2021, Consultation 3 has just closed and is being evaluated by a team of external analysts. This and the previous stage of consultation were the most important. We requested that each committee first submit up to twenty keywords/concepts felt indispensable and desirable in a new definition and next select and assess their preferred terms from the subsequent list that emerged from around the world. The following stages consist of drafting proposals based on the outcome of these processes, translating them as closely as possible into the three official ICOM languages (English, French, and Spanish), and once more submitting these to consultation. Proposals will take Consultations 2 and 3 into consideration, respecting the findings, while incorporating the museological experience and expertise of the twenty members of ICOM Define, who represent a wide array of cultural, linguistic, and professional backgrounds.

Many questions arise. First, how can ICOM's museum definition encompass the diversity of museum practice? Large, small, community, state,

Lauran Bonilla-Merchav and Bruno Brulon Soares

LGBTIQ+, religious, virtual . . . is it even possible to unite these very distinct museums into a single definition? Further, who is the definition for? Is it a legal tool or for museum professionals? Is it prescriptive or aspirational? Should it be precise or open-ended? These are all questions that ICOM Define does not intend to answer on its own. Rather, we have designed a process of listening to what committees consider necessary in a new definition. There are no right answers, and there will never be total agreement. Instead, we are inspired by the words of Bonita Bennet, director for eleven years of the District Six Museum in Cape Town: "We prefer to explore processes that are premised on the existence of divergent views, assuming that complete consensus will never be achieved nor be desirable."[11]

Museum professionals are a heterogenous community linked through their work with heritage, and a new definition must be borne out of the diversity of this community, rather than be the result of a particular vision imposed upon it. In coalescing as many views as possible, the challenge and the aim, perhaps unreachable, is to succinctly explain what all museums have in common everywhere.

ICOM Define has pursued a participatory process with its community. By listening to this varied body and trusting it to help create a new proposal, the goal is to arrive at a definition that more aptly pertains and belongs to the membership, better reflecting what they dedicate their lives to. Through active engagement and connection, it is conceivable that the new definition proposal may better fit the global community of museum professionals. Although not all have participated, a process was facilitated that enabled every committee to contribute. The methodology thus aims to construct a new definition using keywords and concepts, proposed and agreed upon by a majority of participating committees, as building blocks toward a defining statement of our shared but very diverse practice.

If, in fact, a new museum definition were to be more specific about social responsibility, then the question is whether it would change museums that aren't already influencers. Would they do things differently? And, might museum relevance increase with a new definition? There is no way of knowing, but it is worth the pursuit. ICOM's museum definition has increasingly set a standard of museum practice in different parts of the world, entering into legislation in some cases and serving as a basis for cultural policies in others.[12] At this point, what the new definition proposal will look like is unknown, but it may, in fact, lead professionals toward greater awareness of the issues to overcome and bring about museum practice that has a wider-reaching impact on society.

Museums have always been changing entities, since the days of private collections and cabinets of curiosities, to the creation of large state museums, the insertion of narrative, and the inclusion of a direct social role. Museology and museography have evolved with the incorporation of thinking and practice in the branches of eco, community, new, social, critical, and experimental museology, all of which are directly impacted by the particular contexts in which they arise. So, can museum professionals from around the world, and from the vast array of museums that exist, agree what their common job is?

Responding to this is nearly impossible, considering the heterogeneity of the field; and the task of trying to do so, some suggest, is superfluous at a time when definitions are considered essentialist and limiting. Yet the definition is important, not only within the statutes of ICOM but as a reference point used by other organizations and governing bodies. It also serves as a benchmark for museums and museum professionals globally. Thus, ICOM's work to create a new definition that can better unite and drive the profession in the twenty-first century, although incredibly challenging, is significant, may yield a greater impact on society, and ultimately needs to be done.

NOTES

1. "Recommendation Concerning the Protection and Promotion of Museums and Collections, Their Diversity and Their Role in Society," UNESCO (2015), https://unesdoc.unesco.org/ark:/48223/pf0000245176.page=14.
2. For a brief history of ICOM in the twentieth century, see Sid Ahmed Baghli, Patrick Boylan, and Yani Herreman, *History of ICOM (1946-1996)* (Paris: ICOM, 1998).
3. "Resolution No. 1 'On Sustainability and the Adoption of Agenda 2030, Transforming Our World,'" ICOM (2019), https://icom.museum/wp-content/uploads/2019/09/Resolutions_2019_EN.pdf.
4. "History of ICOM," ICOM, https://icom.museum/en/about-us/history-of-icom/.
5. Jette Sandahl, "Addressing Societal Responsibilities through Core Museum Functions and Methods: The Museum Definition, Prospects and Potentials," *Museum International* 71, nos. 281-82 (2019): iv-v.
6. For more information on the work done by MDPP and the parameters upon which the definition proposals were based, see Jette Sandahl, "The Museum Definition as the Backbone of ICOM," *Museum International* 71, nos. 281-82 (2019): 1-9. For the five definitions submitted to the executive board and an explanation of how these were generated, see MDPP, "Submission to the Executive Board, according to decision by the EB, December 2018, of five different proposals for a new museum definition, for a final selection by the EB," ICOM (July 2019).
7. The 2019 proposed definition reads as follows: "Museums are democratizing, inclusive and polyphonic spaces for critical dialogue about the pasts and the futures. Acknowledging and addressing the conflicts and challenges of the present, they hold artefacts and specimens in trust for society, safeguard diverse memories for future generations and guarantee equal rights and equal access to heritage for all people. Museums are not for profit. They are participatory and transparent, and work in active partnership with and for diverse communities to collect, preserve, research, interpret, exhibit, and enhance understandings of the world, aiming to contribute to human dignity and social justice, global equality and planetary wellbeing."
8. Alex Marshall, "What Is a Museum? A Dispute Erupts over a New Definition," *New York Times*, August 6, 2020, https://www.nytimes.com/2020/08/06/arts/what-is-a-museum.html.

9. Of particular importance within this debate are the variety of perspectives presented in the *Museum International* volume of 2019 dedicated to the subject, as well as the multiple ICOFOM publications dedicated to the subject available on their website, https://icofom.mini.icom.museum/publications-2/the-monographs-of-icofom/#.
10. See the evolution of the ICOM definition in André Desvallées and François Mairesse, eds., "Museum," in *Dictionnaire encyclopédique de muséologie* (Paris: Armand Colin, 2011).
11. Bonita Bennett, "Introduction: District Six Museum: Activists for Change," *Museum International*, 271–72 (2016): 5–10.
12. Michele Rivet, "La définition du musée: Que nous disent les droits nationaux?," in *Définir le Musée du XXIème Siècle*, ed. François Mairesse (Paris: ICOFOM, 2017), 53–123, http://icofom.mini.icom.museum/wp-content/uploads/sites/18/2018/12/LIVRE_FINAL_DEFINITION_Icofom_Definition_couv_cahier.pdf.

20

Redefine the Museum

MAKING A CASE FOR EMBRACING OUR INNER AGENT OF CHANGE

Lisa Sasaki

One afternoon I found myself on an airplane on my way to a job interview. Striking up a conversation with the person sitting next to me, who happened to be a longtime resident of the city where I was interviewing, I decided to find out a bit more about the museum from her perspective. "Oh, I love that museum!" she exclaimed. That's a good sign, I thought, until she continued: "I've been there twice—once when I was in fourth grade and again a couple of years ago when I had relatives in town."

I have heard variations of this same story since I started working at museums more than twenty-five years ago: museums as wonderful places for a field trip or special places to visit when you have out-of-town guests or are on vacation but not necessarily a part of everyday life. This assumption about museums' role within American society—a "nice to have" rather than a "need to have"—unfortunately places most institutions on the path of stagnating attendance, questionable long-term sustainability, and skepticism about their overall ability to address contemporary issues. Like all organisms and organizations, museums must also evolve or risk irrelevancy and extinction. Through crisis and economic downturns, institutions are discovering that they can no longer exist within the delicate ecosystem of society merely as cabinets of curiosity or temples on the hill. Whether or not it is acknowledged, they have a shared commitment, responsibility, and authority in relationship to their communities.

How then can museums chronicle the past while also participating in the present and the future of the communities they serve? What does it mean for museums to have influence in meaningful ways, during both times of need and daily life? Specifically, can museums truly be agents of change within their communities after a legacy of neutrality and separateness?

I know that many of us who work in museums like to think that we already contribute to our communities through what we currently do—scholarship, collections care, exhibition, interpretation, and, over the past several decades, a focus on education. The true test, however, comes when we turn our gaze outward rather than inward to measure our impact, looking at not just the number of artifacts in our collections or the exhibitions we produce each year but also the number of lives we change outside our walls. Do museums and the work that we do as museum workers affect people in their day-to-day lives in a direct and lasting way? Are museums truly vital to our audiences and communities?

The shuttering of buildings for months due to the 2020 global COVID-19 pandemic combined with the racial justice reckoning following the murder of George Floyd was a rare opportunity for museums to step away from the never-ending cycle of exhibitions, programs, and object care to ask themselves these questions and examine the role that museums have traditionally held. Are we satisfied with being "America's attic," or what I like to call the "castor oil of society," something that is kept in the medicine cabinet for the vague reason that we were once told it was good for us but soon found it replaceable with other, more efficient items? Even as museums wrestled with transforming themselves digitally with their physical spaces closed, a "new normal" required museums to take a deep look at themselves.

But questioning decades—even centuries—of what many people believe to be the inalienable role of museums can be a challenge. When called upon, how do we embrace our inner agent of change, both for our institutions and our communities? After spending years working in community-based museums and watching museum staff struggle with how to answer these questions, I can recommend a few fundamental places to start (or continue) our redefinition of what it means to be a museum.

PUT PEOPLE FIRST

Inevitably, when questioning the role of museums and proposing the addition of community responsibility and responsiveness to the definition of what a museum is, some of my colleagues immediately protested, "But we're not a social service organization or a community center!" My response to this statement has always been, "Why not?" Understanding, of course, that museums do not necessarily have the infrastructure or knowledge to distribute public services in the same manner as organizations for which that is their primary function, museums have no reason why they cannot embrace a service mentality.

In fact, a subset of museums has already done this. From the earliest "pay what you can" programs to actively challenging long-held museum practice by encouraging visitors to "please touch," children's museums have operated easily on the dividing line between museums, communities, and service. According to the Association of Children's Museums (ACM), one of the fundamental pillars that define all children's museums, no matter their size, is to be an advocate for children and to respond to the needs of children and families in their communities. This role is even more apparent during times of crisis. ACM's pandemic response initiative, Museums Mobilize, saw a trend among participating museums—seventy-eight children's museums in thirty-four states and four countries—to develop programming to combat food insecurity, including the creation of museum-based food pantries when they realized that families were reluctant or even fearful of going to food banks.[1]

What has allowed children's museums in particular to embrace their role as advocate and move into areas of need while traditional museums continue to hesitate? The answer to this question can be found in what—or who—they choose to center their institutions around. I once had the opportunity to visit the Children's Museum of Tacoma. In 2019, the museum announced that it was formally embracing an expanded role: "The work of the Children's Museum of Tacoma has evolved and grown over the last decade. We are an education and advocacy organization that has become more than a museum."[2]

Prior to this announcement, I heard their staff talk about how, when they realized that children were arriving hungry to their museum because they did not have food at home, they began offering breakfast as a part of the program. Then, when the staff realized that the same children were going home to a place where there was not enough food, they figured out a way to send meals home so that the entire family could eat. When I asked the museum's director how she was able to get her board and stakeholders to support what sounded an awful lot like a social service, her response was, to paraphrase, "It was easy because fundamentally as a children's museum, we understand that museums are about people. When you start from there, everything else is easy."

The examples that the Children's Museum of Tacoma and other children's museums provide should be noted not only because of the many children and families whose lives are made better through their work but because they are also a reminder that museum professionals need to remember not just *what* we do but *why* we do it, and *for whom*. When we place people first—rather than objects or scholarship, no matter how worthy—museums have so many more possibilities of what they can and should do. When we place people at the center of what museums do, we naturally start to question our core functions and can better prioritize where the resources at our disposal should go.

INTERROGATE OUR MISSIONS

This type of recentering around who museums serve rather than what we do leads the conversation back to the missions and visions under which museums operate. I am not so radical as to recommend dismissing what so many people see to be the primary functions of most museums, which typically includes some combination and variation of exhibition, collection, scholarship, and interpretation. I would advocate, however, for museums to interrogate our missions and visions of the future with one simple question: To what end? To what end do we exhibit, preserve, study, educate? Are we doing these things simply because that is what we have always done? Or is there another, deeper purpose that these actions serve? Finally, if museums commit to placing people first, should we not mention who we serve in our mission and vision statements?

As a member of the leadership team at the Oakland Museum of California (OMCA), in 2015 I participated in an examination of its mission and vision statements as a part of strategic planning. The mission and vision that were in place at that time were perfectly serviceable: OMCA's mission was to connect communities to the cultural and environmental heritage of California, and its vision was to be a dynamic place of learning and connection where the public discovers, explores, and celebrates the California experience. When the question of "To what end?" was applied, however, the team had to wrestle with what measurable outcomes would happen if the museum connected communities to this heritage and, more important, who exactly were the communities that the statements were referencing.

The team ultimately realized that the result we were hoping to achieve was for the museum to play a role in helping Oakland thrive. OMCA's mission now is to inspire all Californians to create a more vibrant future for themselves and their communities. Its vision of the future is one where OMCA is the heart of a thriving community and achieves leadership in the field through an exemplary commitment to and impact on its surrounding neighborhoods. What exactly that impact would look like and how it would be measured took several more years to determine, a process outlined by OMCA's deputy director Kelly McKinley in the article "What Is Our Museum's Social Impact: Trying to Understand and Measure How Our Museum Changes Lives in Our Community."[3] Following that process, OMCA now measures its impact by looking at metrics that quantify an increased sense of welcome, belonging, and connection between people who are from different backgrounds. For example, how many visitors valued hearing ideas different from their own at OMCA (92 percent) and how many visitors appreciate that OMCA tells stories from different communities (95 percent).[4]

OMCA is just one of many museums refining their purpose through their mission and vision statements, from small museums ("Together with local communities, the Anacostia Community Museum illuminates and amplifies our collective power. As a trusted and inclusive center, the [museum] seeks to inspire communities to take action, and is an incubator for the next generation of civically engaged citizens.")[5] to midsize museums ("Burke Museum cares for and shares natural and cultural collections so all people can learn, be inspired, generate knowledge, feel joy, and heal")[6] to large multi-museum complexes (the Natural History Museums of Los Angeles' vision is "to inspire wonder, discovery, and responsibility for our natural and cultural worlds")[7]. These efforts prove that museums can move beyond the vague and indistinct words that have defined missions and visions in the past and toward words that articulate action, change, and shared responsibility.

GO BEYOND OUR WALLS AND COMFORT ZONES

For generations, a museum's purpose has been defined primarily by what was produced within the walls of the museum. Near constant advances in technology, however, have opened the museum to visitors, researchers, and communities who may never visit its physical building. The COVID-19 pandemic further accelerated this trend, with museums pivoting to producing digital content for a world stuck at home. Programs and processes that museum staff once swore were reliant upon an in-person museum experience were suddenly happening online, oftentimes with far greater reach than the IRL (in real life) equivalent.

Beyond providing more digital content, what if museums were no longer tethered to the four walls of a gallery or building? What if museums could leave their comfort zones both physically and philosophically in service to community? The Smithsonian's Anacostia Community Museum (ACM), one of the oldest community museums in the United States, founded by John Kinard in 1967, has tested this idea numerous times. One example is its "offsite and in the city" activities that saw the museum doing programs in local cafés and storefronts, places where residents of Washington, D.C.'s, Wards 7 and 8 felt comfortable rather than expecting them to always trek to the museum. More recently, ACM reimagined two of its exhibitions, *Men of Change: Taking It to the Streets* and *Food for the People: Eating and Activism in Greater Washington*. Slated for its gallery, instead they became outdoor installations in the Deanwood neighborhood and the museum's outdoor plaza, respectively, so they would be safely accessible to the community during the pandemic.

Another example of stretching beyond boundaries is ACM's partnership with Feed the Fridge. The motto of Feed the Fridge is "Nutrition with Dignity," and the organization aims to solve hunger by turning "food insecurity" into "meal security" through free restaurant-prepared meals placed in twenty-two refrigerators in recreation centers, schools, and other areas around the District of Columbia where residents can access them through a dignified experience, no questions asked. Placing a refrigerator in the parking lot of a Smithsonian museum was definitely outside the institution's comfort zone; however, the museum staff persevered, working through every protocol and risk mitigation. Within six months, the refrigerator in ACM's parking lot was one of the most highly used refrigerators in the system, distributing more than seven thousand meals while requiring little expenditure or work from the museum other than the use of an electrical outlet and a partnership agreement.

Even if a museum is not quite ready to embrace new practices focused on service and community care, challenging ourselves to go beyond physical locations and pushing at the edges of institutional comfort zones does not fundamentally change a museum's purpose. Rather, this can expand and enhance

Figure 20.1. The outdoor *Food for the People: Eating and Activism in Greater Washington* exhibition at the Smithsonian's Anacostia Community Museum. *Courtesy of the Anacostia Community Museum. Photo by Samir Meghelli, curator*

it, opening museums to new audiences and demonstrating to the public that they are worth the effort. Like any good host will know, people eventually stop accepting your invitations if you constantly refuse opportunities to join them where they are and if you are not willing to try to contest practices that limit meaningful interactions.

ACCEPT ACCOUNTABILITY

For those hoping to weather what they would consider the "latest fad" in the museum field to quietly continue their "old normal," I must warn that accountability to those we serve looks very different today. In the past, as long as they avoided the rare headline-making scandal, museums could demonstrate their stewardship of public and private funds simply through audited financials and adherence to ethics around collecting and collections care. Today, social media provides a platform for staff and constituents alike to question museums' activities—or lack thereof—and news outlets have been quick to point out museums' late arrival on the scene, as in Holland Cotter's *New York Times* article "Museums Are Finally Taking a Stand. But Can They Find Their Footing?"

Figure 20.2. Feed the Fridge at the Smithsonian's Anacostia Community Museum offers free meals through a dignified experience. *Courtesy of the Anacostia Community Museum. Photo by Willette Matthews*

Holland critiqued how museums rushed to support Black Lives Matter in the months following the killing of George Floyd, responding with gestures that "felt both self-aggrandizing and too little too late." He ended his article by noting, "The state of emergency we're in won't last forever. News cycles roll on; people get distracted. But anyone can see that after these torturous months and weeks, we're in a new place, a new phase of social history. Our museums should be ready to record it and preserve it, and be part of it."[8] Holland also articulated several excellent recommendations on what museum leaders could do beyond promising future change, including listening to communities when they say what they need, restructuring internally and hiring diverse staff, and rewriting the stories that the collections tell, multiple times if required. I would add that leaders also need to understand that refusing to address societal issues and their institution's contributions to them is more damaging than trying and perhaps misstepping along the way.

Even more problematic is putting out statements of solidarity or inclusion without corresponding actions to support those statements. Change the Museum (@changethemuseum), an account on Instagram, features anonymous posts from museum professionals collected for the purpose of "pressuring

US museums to move beyond lip service proclamations by amplifying tales of unchecked racism." This is one example of how social media have created new and very public mechanisms for accountability. Although some people have questioned whether the anonymous—as well as what could be considered the publicly shaming—nature of these posts will really lead to lasting organizational change, the takeaway for museums should be that they need to understand that they now stand accountable for their inaction just as much as for their actions.

REDEFINE MUSEUM

So, I come back to the question I posed: whether, after a legacy of neutrality and separateness, museums can truly add "agent of change" and "influencer" to the collective definition of a museum. I believe that museums can. But only if we—the people who work within, volunteer for, provide leadership and funding for, or simply just love museums—embrace our own inner change agent and see the people we serve not just as the number of bodies through the door but as our main duty, as articulated in our vision and mission statements. And only if we get beyond our self-imposed walls and accept that our inactions speak more loudly than our words in public statements or diversity and inclusion plans. Only then can we claim some small right to the trust and influence within the communities to which museums belong.

One day I hope we will no longer need to question or challenge the fact that the definition of museums has shifted. One day I hope when I sit next to someone on an airplane and I ask about their local museum, their answer will be, "Why, yes, I was just there the other day, and I can't imagine what I'd do without it."

NOTES

1. "Museums in a Pandemic: Impacts for Workforce and Audiences & Partners," Association of Children's Museums, https://childrensmuseums.org/2021/04/26/museums-in-a-pandemic-impacts-for-workforce-and-audiences-partners/.
2. What Is Greentrike?, https://greentrike.org/.
3. Kelly McKinley, "What Is Our Museum's Social Impact: Trying to Understand and Measure How Our Museum Changes Lives in Our Community," *Medium* (2017), https://medium.com/new-faces-new-spaces/what-is-our-museums-social-impact-62525fe88d16.
4. OMCA Impact Report, https://museumca.org/about-omca?qt-mission_history_central=1#qt-mission_history_central.
5. Our Mission, Smithsonian Anacostia Community Museum, https://anacostia.si.edu/About?showFull=1.
6. Our Mission, Burke Museum, https://www.burkemuseum.org/about.
7. Strategic Framework, Natural History Museums of Los Angeles County, https://nhmlac.org/about-us/strategic-framework-nhmlac.
8. Holland Cotter, "Museums Are Finally Taking a Stand. But Can They Find Their Footing?," *New York Times*, June 11, 2020, https://www.nytimes.com/2020/06/11/arts/design/museums-protests-race-smithsonian.html.

Part Six

Crisis

ENVIRONMENTALISM, SUSTAINABILITY, AND MUSEUMS

21

Beyond Crisis

MUSEUMS AND SUSTAINABILITY

William Underwood Eiland

The series of conversations that gave rise to the various discussion points of this volume emanated from the quest for a definition of "museum" that is universally acceptable. Consequently, among the suggested descriptive terms that characterize museums, one in particular, although in itself needing further precision of meaning, springs above the others to reach the status of crisis: sustainability, which we shall define as does the Office of Sustainability at the University of Georgia: "Acknowledging historical and varied uses of the term, our current working definition of sustainability . . . is 'The just and ethical integration of social, environmental, and economic solutions to ensure that all people can thrive, both now and in the future.'" But to this definition, with its admirable scope, we must add the cultural dimension that is of equal or higher importance for museums.

Any doubts that, as integral parts of the social construct, museums are in crisis should be dispelled by news of devastating fires in California, floods in New Jersey, killingly high temperatures in the Midwest, food insecurity throughout the nation, and increasingly destructive weather patterns, all of which have jeopardized museum collections, buildings, and the lives and safety of staff and visitors. The news from abroad is no less unsettling. Mother Earth seems to be taking her revenge for perennial mistreatment and neglect. Moreover, social problems and economic disparity, immigration policy and displacement are worldwide issues, not restricted to any one country or region. Hunger, for example, directly related to drought, is ravaging parts of Africa.

Just as in society at large, so, too, in museums exists some disagreement about their social and environmental role. The crises in which museums find themselves are far-reaching and demand responses to complicated and urgent issues, several of which fall under the rubric of sustainability.

In the newsletter of the International Council of Museums (ICOM) of October 2021, its president, Alberto Garlandini, asserts that the current, abiding concern for the organization is the future of museums and "their activities for sustainability and climate justice." In his words, these are crucial, exigent issues for the international community of museums, at a critical time when "global challenges call for global responses" and when museums cannot, ostrich-like, bury their heads in sand too shallow to hide from the perilous state of the planet and the social and economic consequences of such pernicious disregard. Among the latter are homelessness and immigration, dependence on fossil fuels, and threats to humankind's universal heritage.

At the Youth4Climate summit at the end of September 2021, Pope Francis praised the gathering of young environmentalists for their activism, especially for "challenging global leaders to make good on promises to curb emissions and insisting that political leaders make wise decisions to promote 'a culture of responsible sharing.'"[1] At roughly the same time, President Lawrence Bacow of Harvard University announced that, through its management company, which oversees a $41 billion endowment, Harvard plans to phase out its legacy fossil fuel investments.[2] The MacArthur Foundation, in its declaration that it would begin divesting from fossil fuels, unambiguously and clearly stated: "Climate change is likely the greatest existential threat to our planet and our collective well-being. With each major scientific report on climate change, the news is more worrisome, not less. Charitable foundations like ours must use all the tools at our disposal to ensure it does not get worse." Museums are such charitable organizations, as well. The museum community's peer professional associations need to heed the MacArthur Foundation's example, at least to the extent of urging its members to look carefully at not only their own endowments and how they are invested but also at ways to reduce carbon emissions and wasteful practices at their home institutions.

The MacArthur Foundation's decision is particularly resonant with the social mission of today's museums:

> The climate crisis affects everyone in the world, but not equally. From wildfires that consume precious forests and rip through communities; to super-storms that inundate homes with floodwaters and ravage infrastructure; and water shortage and droughts that destroy crops and livelihoods—we see the ways in which some communities, many already marginalized, are suffering more from the ravages of climate change than others.[3]

The focus of this publication—*What Is a Museum?*—responds to many of these concerns, but surely overriding them all, and contributing mightily to the very

William Underwood Eiland

conditions museums are trying to correct, is the sustainability of the planet, presently in a condition of universal and desperate alarm.

The three articles noted above, along with several others, arrived on my desk on the same day. Such is the news, the apprehension, even the attempts to be proactive in meeting this peril. Museums play a crucial role in both the cultural and civic life of their communities, and, therefore, have the responsibility to call out, to bear witness to, and to respond to the further degradation of the planet and the wanton waste of its resources. That joining of civic and social obligations may indeed fall under the heading of sustainability, with museums of all types in the forefront of practices that reduce our carbon footprint, that help repair the damage done to our joint home—this planet and all its denizens—and that educate the global citizenry to the urgency of action. Scientists must not have the sole voice in decrying the slow pace of remediation or, in fact, finding the solutions to the increasingly severe effects of climate change and the irrevocable pairing of sustainability in its broadest sense with the more specific and immediate concerns of the smaller or midsize museum with the maintenance of its operations through wise and imaginative attention to its fiscal and human resources. In other words, as equally threatened members of the global community, museums must share responsibility for providing leadership, for strengthening resources, and for protecting natural systems in peril. Given the severity of the threats to our environment, no museum—history, science, art, or others—is exempt from this mandate.

In his "Presidential Proclamation on National Arts and Humanities Month" in October 2021, President Joe Biden linked the planet's sustainability to the other perils with which it is plagued: "As our nation continues to grapple with consequential crises—from combating the ongoing global pandemic and addressing cries for social justice to tackling the existential threat that climate change poses to our planet—the arts and humanities enable us to both understand our experiences and lift our sights."

As a member of ICOM's Working Group on Sustainability, Morien Rees has emphasized that museums are not exempt from an active response to the global crises, social, economic, and, to be sure, environmental, that are urgent and increasing in severity. He finds that, although other issues, as identified in this volume, are of immediate importance to museums, institutions must prioritize direct action in combating climate change and, as a collateral obligation, must lead by example and disseminate information about the crisis, especially in joining in the implementation of the United Nations' Transforming Our World: The 2030 Agenda for Sustainable Development and in support of its seventeen sustainability goals.[4] Without a firm commitment to sustainability, Rees argues, other issues of concern to museums lack the context, the imperative, the "frame," as he puts it, for resolution. He succinctly emphasizes that sustainability is the most important and challenging crisis for museums now and for the foreseeable future, and that, consequently, a new museum definition, a revision of ICOM's code of ethics, and the ten-year strategic plan all must reflect the "foundational" framework of sustainability. For Rees, the encompassing imperative for museums, indeed for humankind, is to repair "our broken relationships with the Earth."

Lisa Yun Lee avers that climate change, especially global warming, is the result of "interdependent, perhaps braided systems of capitalism, patriarchy and the commodification of nature, militarism, imperialism, and settler colonialism."[5] Because of the history of oppression and continuing systemic racism, she argues, the human right to decent and affordable housing makes of her museum, the National Public Housing Museum, a site of conscience. Her description of her museum's educational and activist mission is already in line with Agenda 2030, whose very preamble links climate change to poverty and to the abrogation of basic human rights, such as housing.

Lee maintains that it would be ironic to call on marginalized people who are "systematically oppressed within our institutions," to confront the climate crisis; she prefers to address all visitors to her museum and to similar sites as "global citizens," rather than as persons living on the outer edge of a "monoculture."

Sarah Sutton describes herself as a "fervent believer that museums are the absolute best partner in addressing climate change," with all the resources at their disposal to do so. In other words, she enjoins museums in what she believes is not only an obligation but also a challenge, one that demands that museums find collaborators in the important work of reducing humankind's carbon imprint. Museums have much to offer partners in this work: their staffs, their objects, their cultural and scientific histories, and, as with every project, fund-raisers. One important way in which museums will be most effective in cooperating with other entities is in the implementation of the seventeen sustainable development goals of the 2030 Agenda. She stresses the urgency of reducing global warming and, thus, limiting climate change.

Greenhouse gas emissions are the villains here, especially the burning of fossil fuels, and Sutton argues that if we are relentless in our insistence on the reduction to 50 percent, then we shall be able to reduce the impact of burning fossil fuels to zero by 2050, thus holding global warming to one and a half degrees.

Museums can begin with looking at their own buildings and how they can reduce such emissions as soon as possible. She agrees that sustainable practice brings with it for the individual museum the ability to resolve or to treat imaginatively other issues, such as food insecurity, health, clean water, and poverty. Every museum of whatever stripe will have to decide the extent to which it will involve itself in issues of economic inequities or social entrepreneurship, even for art museums, for example, the extent to which they believe their mission includes addressing such issues. Sutton encourages each museum to measure the impact of climate warming on its building, its collections, its activities, and, especially, its audiences, to whom museums, through educational programs and exhibitions, should be offering climate literacy.

Were one to search the dictionary for a suitable definition of crisis, one would find, among others, "a time or state of affairs requiring prompt or decisive action."[6] This volume and the webinar that preceded it underline the importance of definitions, especially of the word "museum," but also of the words "sustainability" and even "crisis." Another word, helpful perhaps in these discussions, is the "braid" all three essayists reference as binding climate change to social and economic issues, with repercussions especially for such cultural agencies as museums, which are in the business of educating audiences. No one, it appears, argues that the COVID-19 pandemic, the social justice movement, and climate emergencies are not intertwined and represent crises for museums that require "prompt" and "decisive action."

In September 2021, however, the Pew Research Center released a report that holds some hope for those of us who are skeptical or see futility in international accord on responses to global warming and concomitant environmental disasters. Although their study found that "many doubt success of international efforts to reduce global warming," they also found that, per the title of the study, "In Response to Climate Change, Citizens in Advanced Economies Are Willing to Alter How They Live and Work." Although many of Pew's respondents feared that climate change would harm them during their lifetimes, many also indicated that "they were willing to change how they live and work to reduce climate change."[7] Of note were the findings that neither the United States nor China received general approbation for their handling of climate change.

The environmental crisis is real; it requires urgent responses. And museums, if for no other reason than self-protection, cannot stand aside and hope that some other agency or government will ameliorate the exigency or resolve it altogether. For all the issues raised and discussed in this volume, none is more urgent than climate change. Museum professionals can take heart, however, and join with the United Nations' declaration that "we are determined to ensure that all human beings can enjoy prosperous and fulfilling lives and that economic, social and technological progress occurs in harmony with nature."[8]

NOTES

1. Associated Press, "Climate Activists Praised by Pope," *Athens Banner Herald*, September 30, 2021, 3A.
2. "Harvard Moves toward Divestment. What's Next?," *Inside Higher Ed*, September 23, 2021, https://www.harvard.edu/president/news/2021/climate-change-update-on Harvard-action/.
3. MacArthur Foundation, "Aligning Our Investments with Our Mission, Values, and Programs," September 26, 2021, https://www.macfound.org/press/perspectives /aligning-our-investments-with-our-mission-values-and-programs.
4. For a discussion of Agenda 2030 and its advancement by ICOM, see Henry MGhie, "ICOM Kyoto 2019: Curating Sustainable Futures through Museums," September

14, 2019, https://curatingtomorrow236646048.wordpress.com. For the seventeen goals of the agenda, see United Nations, Department of Economic and Social Affairs, Sustainable Development, "Transforming Our World: The 2030 Agenda for Sustainable Development," https://sdgs.un.org/2030agenda. In the preamble, the agenda also marries social and economic issues to sustainability: "We recognize that eradicating poverty in all its forms and dimensions, including extreme poverty, is the greatest global challenge and an indispensable requirement for sustainable development."

5. "What Is a Museum? An Exploration in Six Parts; Part 5: Crisis: Environmentalism, Sustainability, and Museums," webinar, International Council of Museums, United States, https://www.icomus.org/webinar-series--part-five.
6. *Merriam-webster.com Dictionary*, s.v. "crisis."
7. James Bell, Jacob Poushter, Moira Fagan, and Christine Huang, "In Response to Climate Change, Citizens in Advanced Economies Are Willing to Alter How They Live and Work," Pew Research Center, September 14, 2021.
8. United Nations, Department of Economic and Social Affairs, Sustainable Development, "Transforming Our World: The 2030 Agenda for Sustainable Development."

22

Imagining Another World at the National Public Housing Museum

Lisa Yun Lee

In order to address the impending climate crisis, we must be willing to imagine another world. This world must be one where everybody can see themselves in order to be ready and willing to fight for it. We must, therefore, acknowledge that global warming has its roots entangled in histories that are too often unacknowledged in our museums: the stolen land our buildings occupy; the enslaved people who created the wealth in the Global North; the provenance of art and artifacts pillaged in the ravages of war; and the continuing systems of racism that institutionalize inequality.

In other words, the climate crisis cannot be understood or addressed solely through policies and actions that regulate carbon emissions; they must also include an analysis of and efforts to reparate the histories of racialized capitalism, imperialism, patriarchy, and settler colonialism. Admittedly, this can seem like a lot. How much can one museum do in the face of so much injustice? At the National Public Housing Museum (NPHM), we are doing this one story at a time.

I begin, therefore, with a land acknowledgment to recognize the Indigenous people who have stewarded the land we occupy in the United States:

> The National Public Housing Museum is located in Chicago, a city whose name is derived from the Algonquian name, which means "river with shores lined with wild leeks." Chicago is home to many Indigenous nations, including the Ojibwe, the Odawa, and the Potawatomi people. Many other tribes, such as the Miami, Ho-Chunk, Menominee, Sac, and Fox, also called this area home.

Following the settler violence, culminating in the Black Hawk War of 1832 and the 1833 treaty of Chicago, many Indigenous people were forcibly removed from these territories or killed. Over a century later, under a different set of government policies (the Indian Relocation Act of 1956), many Indigenous nations found themselves once again coerced to move—this time, back to the urban centers where their ancestors were originally dispossessed. Today, Chicago has the third-largest urban Indigenous population in the United States, with more than sixty-five thousand Native Americans in the greater metropolitan area who continue to care for the land and waterways.

Chicago was also the home of the first non-Native American naturalized citizen of the Potawatomi people—Jean Baptiste Point du Sable—who lived with his beloved wife, Kitihawa, a Potawatomi woman, after their marriage in 1770. Following her displacement during the Trail of Tears, du Sable followed her to Iowa, where they raised their family and spent the rest of their lives.

As a museum professional and cultural activist, I strive to remember and understand this violent history and honor this place we inhabit.

When you talk to many scientists, they will tell you about the dangers of monocultures for our soil and planet. We live in a world where 80,000 edible plants could be used for food, yet only about 150 are cultivated, and just eight are traded globally. The same can be said about homogeneity for democracy. There are more than 6,500 living languages, although 43 percent are endangered, and only 12 languages are spoken regularly across borders. There are also more than 12,583 distinct ethnic groups and more than 19 major religions. This diversity is not a "problem" to be solved but the very essence of life on this planet.

Museums should not simply "celebrate" diversity. They must actively dismantle systems such as White supremacy—which homogenize, "whitewash," and erase difference—in order to create vibrant programs, capacious exhibits, and equitable relationships that preserve, interpret, and tell the most varied and inclusive stories.

NPHM is the only cultural institution dedicated to telling the stories of public housing in the United States. The museum was founded in the wake of urban renewal policies that collectively dismantled and destroyed the largest number of affordable housing units in history—albeit in efforts to address crumbling buildings, racial poverty, and segregation, which are deeply connected with systems of environmental racism.

During this period in Chicago, under what was called the "Plan for Transformation," public housing residents, preservationists, scholars, and advocates came together to demand that one last building of the Jane Addams Homes—a 1937 Public Works Association complex designed by architect John Holabird—be preserved for residents to create a museum where they could contribute to the narrative about the meaning and impact of public housing. It was also to preserve, interpret, and propel the right of all people to a home and fight

Lisa Yun Lee

for housing as a human right. Residents profoundly understood the power of place and the power of self-representation, tenaciously demanding a museum in a historic building that would serve as a visible reminder of the history of public housing. They understood how a cultural institution might be a site for resistance against erasure and forgetting and be useful in their struggle for self-determination.

NPHM is a site of conscience and part of a global network of museums and historic locations committed to the power of place and memory. We insist that in order to preserve history, we must make it relevant to today's most pressing issues. And we cannot solve today's biggest problems without going back in time and asking, What have we not yet learned from the past?

One of the museum's first efforts was a commitment to creating the largest archive of stories of public housing residents. The Oral History Archive is a collection of diverse, compelling stories from people who lived in and contributed to U.S. public housing from the 1930s to the present. The collection includes intimate narratives that bear witness to a U.S. history that is both brilliantly ambitious and deeply troubled. The archive documents the histories of those left out of the mainstream record and inspires listeners to discover stories of hope and resilience where they might have seen only poverty and despair.

NPHM also trains public housing residents to gather stories through a rigorous program that includes ethical interview practices, media skills, and recording techniques. The museum then offers job opportunities through the Oral History Corps to trainees interested in continuing to work with us to build the museum's archive. These rich, nourishing narratives are part of the wealth of our nation and the cultural capital of public housing residents.

"It's always someone else's story first," Rebecca Solnit has written, "and it never stops being their story too, no matter how well you tell it, how widely you spread it."[1] For many decades now, there have been examples of exhibits that are co-curated and envisioned with communities. In the field, we refer to this as the "sharing of authority." When immersing ourselves in this work, we often recognize that we never had authority in the first place. But too often, this basic principle of engagement and inclusion is still the exception and not the rule.

An example of NPHM's exhibition strategy that attempts to honor the authorship and agency of public housing residents is *History Lessons: Everyday Objects from Chicago Public Housing*. The exhibit featured an array of everyday, vernacular objects displayed with labels written by their owners during workshops with author and cultural activist Audrey Petty and poet and teaching artist Nate Marshall, along with several labels based on interviews conducted by photo-historian Richard Cahan. Cahan, who co-organized the exhibit, works in the tradition of Studs Terkel, documenting the day-to-day lives of people as part of a commitment to expand the historical record.

Chicago public housing residents, both past and present, lent twenty-two objects, including Lee Roy "Solid Gold" Murphy's championship boxing belt; the bedazzled leather motorcycle jacket of legendary housing activist and Cabrini-Green Homes organizer Marion Stamps; and Inez Turovitz Medor's lovingly well-worn, wooden gefilte fish bowl, passed down through several generations. These objects span the entire history of Chicago public housing, beginning in 1938 to the present, and tell a beautiful, troubling story.

The decision to feature resident voices in myriad forms, rather than on "tombstone" labels (as they are referred to in museum parlance), consciously challenged and went outside the conventional rectangular box of factual evidence, both metaphorically and literally—which usually interprets artifacts in an objective, omniscient voice. Insistently and unapologetically subjective, these labels, both prose and poetry, were infused with imagination, desire, love, guts, and humor.

History, when told through everyday stories that speak to the affective and emotional truths of lived experience, can be powerful. In a world where marginalized people living in poverty are relegated in most forms of representation—to either achieving extraordinary feats of success, resilience, and survival or being represented as abject failures succumbing to the indignities of life—*History Lessons* reflected the mission of the museum. This includes a commitment to building a foundation of stories that is capacious and inclusive of those who have, too often, been written out of the nation's narrative.

Further, this history, hidden in plain sight, creates an opportunity to understand an often-neglected part of the cultural and political histories that make up vibrant public housing communities. The mundane acts that constitute our existence speak truth to power and give expression to the murmurings of the heart. Historian Robin D. G. Kelley has described this as forms of everyday resistance or "dissident political culture that manifests itself in daily conversations, folklore, jokes, songs, and other cultural practices."[2]

Historians who study the politics of public housing usually emphasize the histories of organized protests, tenant rent strikes, landmark lawsuits, and consent decrees and policy initiatives. However, Kelley's work suggests that many insights are to be gained when we expand the realm of the "political" to include daily acts, including disorganized, unintentional thoughts and actions and incipient feelings that have a cumulative effect on power relations—whether or not intended. And while NPHM passionately believes in reimagining our commonwealth to include the intangible value of preserving, disseminating, and circulating these stories, the museum is also exploring ways of stabilizing the planet by securing a just transition to post-exploitative economies in more tangible ways.

One of our core programs is an Entrepreneurship Hub, which includes a cooperative museum store owned and operated with public housing residents. A working group of museum board members, staff, and residents from across the country have also committed to putting into practice some of the lessons learned from the stories of many resilient, resistant businesses in public hous-

Lisa Yun Lee

ing. These businesses emphasized community interdependence over individual independence and were part of a larger solidarity economy, where ethical values and social profitability were prioritized over individual financial profits. Candy ladies, barbershops, cooperative gardens, and laundry enterprises prioritized the welfare of people and planet over the bottom line and blind growth.

Not many people know, for example, about the Altgeld Cooperative, started by residents of Altgeld Gardens, on the far South Side of Chicago. Founded in September 1944, the cooperative had returned several hundred thousand dollars to customers and stockholders by 1949. With an income of more than $750,000 a year (the equivalent of $6.5 million today), it claimed to be the largest cooperative store in the United States—competing with the prices of large corporate chains nearby and boasting twenty-seven employees with union-scale wages.

From the first land trusts in Mississippi to mutual aid efforts, NPHM is committed to preserving, interpreting, and disseminating these histories to learn important lessons. The museum's T-shirts and tote bags, for example, are printed in the cooperative by youth with whom we share all profits. NPHM is also committed to diversifying the cultural workforces of museums and reimagining the positions that have traditionally been paid and valued the least. Recent studies of museum workers in the United States have provided dismal data about diversity of staff. Twenty-eight percent of museum staff identify as people of color, but 90 percent of this group are the lowest-waged workers. In the United States, valuable movements such as Mass Action and Museum Workers Speak have organized and made contributions that we have much to learn from.

In response to these movements, NPHM has researched the history of the Chicago Housing Authority (CHA) Tenant Patrol, which is considered one of the best examples of self-organization to redefine public safety. In response to the absence of adequate public safety measures, including corrupt, rogue police acting with impunity, the CHA Tenant Patrol program was formed as a citizen's initiative in 1989. Concerned residents such as Akbarali Makani (age seventy-three) and Ruth Artis (age sixty-nine) were involved in maintaining a safe living environment as an alternative to police and state surveillance. They patrolled, observed, addressed hazardous building conditions, watched after children, and conducted wellness checks on the elderly.

At NPHM, our visitor service staff will be modeled on this program, moving away from surveillance tactics and charged and empowered to create spaces for radical generosity and care. The work that makes all other positions possible in museums—from the cleaning staff to the care work of visitor services and those tasked with public safety—has traditionally been underpaid, undervalued, and made invisible in museum social policies. This work should be valued, centered, and a core part of our vision and mission.

Recently, NPHM was called the "Museum of the Future" in an article commissioned by the Pulitzer Center, which also recognized the ways we have responded to the twin viruses of COVID-19 and systemic racism.[3] Moral imperatives demand moral accountability—which requires providing different kinds of accounts and storytelling, as well as alternative types of financial commitments. These variations of responsibility are all linked etymologically, literally, and symbolically. All our efforts are a call to our nation to have a more inclusive foundation for the stories we preserve and tell. Our work includes a commitment to linking storytelling, or the *giving* of accounts, with historical and moral accountability and the equitable distribution of resources, or the *keeping* of accounts.

Just because you grew up in public housing doesn't mean you are able to analyze public housing, so the museum also relies on the research and contributions of an interdisciplinary group of advisers. This consists of some of the nation's most prominent housing scholars, including Lawrence Vale, Rhonda Williams, D. Bradford Hunt, Roberta Feldman, Edward Rothstein, and Mary Pattillo, among many others. However, all our efforts are committed to creating a more participatory democracy in our museum. It doesn't make sense to call on people to use their voices to confront the climate crisis when we know marginalized voices are systematically oppressed within our institutions.

We must engage and address all of our stakeholders as more than just consumers of knowledge; they are also global citizens, creators, and change agents. Unless we tackle systems of exclusion locally, we will continue to undermine the climate solutions we seek. Each museum must find its own way to address the impending devastation of climate change. For NPHM, finding ways to become a civic anchor for our communities and offering creative solutions to reawaken a collective commitment to the public good, along with demands to create a true commonwealth, are all part of the battle to sustain and save a planet worth fighting for.

NOTES

1. Rebecca Solnit, "To Break the Story, You Must Break the Status Quo," *Literary Hub*, May 26, 2016, https://lithub.com/to-break-the-story-you-must-break-the-status-quo/#_ftnref1.
2. Robin D. G. Kelley, *Race Rebels: Culture, Politics, and the Black Working Class* (New York: Free Press, 1994), 8.
3. Carlos Ballesteros, "The Museum of the Future: The National Public Housing Museum Adapts to Covid-19," *Southside Weekly*, July 31, 2020, https://southsideweekly.com/museum-future-national-public-housing-museum-adapts-covid-19/.

Lisa Yun Lee

23

ICOM and Sustainable Futures

ON SUSTAINABILITY AND IMPLEMENTING AGENDA 2030

Morien Rees

As I write this, at the beginning of October 2021, the global media is replete with reports of fire, floods, drought, and melting ice and visualizations of the effect of a rise in sea level on such iconic American sites such as the Space Center Houston, the Santa Monica Pier, and the Lincoln Memorial in Washington, D.C., at 1.5 and 3 degrees of warming.[1] News stories relating the devastating and ongoing effects of climate breakdown abound. Still, denial endures, and political inaction remains the rule. What is notably absent from the discourse are narratives in which local populations around the world can partake, where people can develop stories on how to adapt, on how to live differently in a world that is rapidly changing.

In this essay, I discuss the role of the global museum community in contributing toward a sustainable future through museums' function as locally anchored disseminators and custodians of shared memories.

The United Nations Intergovernmental Panel on Climate Change (IPCC) report, *Climate Change 2021: The Physical Science Basis. Contribution of Working Group I to the Sixth Assessment Report of the Intergovernmental Panel on Climate Change,*[2] states that climate breakdown is unequivocally caused by human activities, prompting the secretary-general of the UN, António Guterres, to call it a "code red for humanity."[3] This was followed by a disquieting report from the International Energy Agency (IEA) in the run-up to the 2021 United Nations Climate Change Conference (COP26) that current plans to cut global carbon emissions will fall 60 percent short of their 2050 net zero target agreed upon under the Paris Agreement.[4] Understandably, a focus is on climate breakdown.

Climate breakdown is the result of a system committed to unlimited growth driven by fossil fuels. The result of unlimited growth within a finite system, such as our planet, is system collapse. The most recent biennial Living Planet Report documents that the average global populations of mammals, birds, fish, amphibians, and reptiles collapsed by 68 percent between 1970 and 2016.[5] We have created an unsustainable world.

Notwithstanding the urgency of addressing climate breakdown or biodiversity loss, these should not distract us from the fundamental truth that to achieve a sustainable future, social, economic, and environmental injustices must all be addressed. Mitigation of and adaption to climate breakdown will necessitate a system change that encompasses each of these three pillars of sustainability. As the IEA writes, achieving net zero emissions by 2050 will require nothing short of the complete transformation of the global energy system.[6]

The international society's response to the urgent, unfolding challenges the planet is facing is not reassuring. Emma Howard Boyd, director of the UK Environmental Agency, in a recent report, stated that "action needs to be integral to government, businesses and communities . . . and people will soon question why it isn't—especially when it is much cheaper to invest early in climate resilience than to live with the costs of inaction."[7] The younger generation, exemplified by the organization Fridays for Future, are also clear in their demands: act now.[8]

Fortuitously, one political framework is in place that addresses these various challenges. In 2015, the 193 countries of the UN General Assembly adopted the 2030 Development Agenda with its seventeen sustainable development goals;[9] its ambition, nothing less than to transform our world. Agenda 2030 is a universal call to action to end poverty, protect the planet, and improve the lives and prospects of everyone, everything, everywhere. Any hope of success in addressing climate breakdown is reliant on *transforming our world* through a transition to a sustainable future predicated on achieving Agenda 2030's goals.

Although social equity, environmental protection and economic viability are described as the three pillars of sustainability, the argument is compelling for adding a fourth: culture.[10] Moreover, within the cultural sphere, much suggests that the museum sector, made up of knowledge institutions and museum practitioners with essential skills in documentation, research, and dissemination, should have an important role to play in achieving sustainable futures. Indeed, it suggests that museums in general have a duty to their communities to prioritize addressing sustainability's three pillars, and ICOM in particular, with its global network of national committees in 122 countries and more than forty thousand members, built on a foundation of a code of ethics, has a singular responsibility in this.

Undeniably, much can be celebrated in the response of individual institutions and museum practitioners worldwide, although in a global perspective the impact is difficult to establish and, more important, little is coordinated. ICOM established the Working Group on Sustainability (WGS) in 2018, in part, in recognition of this challenge. This initiative resulted in a focus on sustainability at the ICOM General Conference in Kyoto in 2019, where the resolution "On Sustainability and Implementing Agenda 2030"[11] was adopted by the General Assembly, aligning the organization with the seventeen goals of the agenda. By choosing sustainability as one of the themes for a second consecutive triennial, in Prague in 2022, the ICOM leadership has given an unequivocal signal to the global museum family of its commitment to attaining a sustainable future.

Henry McGhie, in his booklet "Museums and the Sustainable Development Goals," writes that sustainability in a narrow sense means the ability to last or continue for a long time.[12] However, it has come to have a broader meaning, as mentioned above, weaving connections between the three pillars or three dimensions of sustainability: environment, society, and the economy. The concept of sustainable development has developed from the Brundtland Commission (1987), where it was defined as "development that meets the needs of the present without compromising the ability of future generations to meet their own needs."[13]

The growing use or misuse of the concept of sustainability—greenwashing—notably in advertising but increasingly in political contexts, has resulted in important debates about sustainability and pathways to sustainable futures disappearing down rabbit holes concerned solely with definitions. Although it is important to acknowledge that the principal reason for aligning ICOM with Agenda 2030 in addressing sustainability is to offer the organization a framework for action, it also allows ICOM to avoid debilitating debates on the definition of sustainability.

The ICOM working group is now in its second mandate period,[14] where its mission is to implement the resolution from Kyoto throughout ICOM, its committees, alliances, affiliated organizations, and Secretariat; and to assist ICOM in becoming carbon neutral by 2050 at the latest, preferably much sooner. The WGS functions as a hub within ICOM, engaged in all matters pertaining to sustainability and climate change, or in the words of the Kyoto resolution, "Empowering the museum family, our visitors and our communities to help secure a sustainable future for all the inhabitants of the planet, human and non-human."

The WGS's practical response has been to identify, broadly speaking, two lines of approach: how ICOM itself can address sustainability within the organization, including technical operations; and how ICOM can assist its public in attaining a sustainable future through dissemination strategies and cross-sector cooperation.

In addressing these two approaches, the global nature of the working group—its members are from all regions of the world—has underlined the differing regional emphases on the various aspects of sustainability: in the Global South, concerns are often linked to social and economic injustice. We need to look no further than the COVID-19 inoculation rates[15] to begin to appreciate the injustice that is at the core of the system that has also created the unsustainable world we live in. The pandemic equally reminds us that remedies are to be found in global agreements such as Agenda 2030 and its imperative to *leave no one behind*.

As the challenges facing the planet grow, and the urgency of addressing them more becomes more apparent, the working group has experienced a concomitant increased demand for action from the ICOM membership—and from the museum sector and civil society outside ICOM, suggesting the need to prioritize the sustainability hub as a central element within ICOM, with greater responsibility for, and accessibility to, the whole membership, together with the resources, human and financial, necessary to fulfill such a task.

Prioritizing how to address the escalating global crises is something that all levels of society—governments, the private business sector, civil society, and individuals—must address, and not in the future, but now. The museum sector is no exception. In recent years, it has increasingly recognized the duty of care owed to its visitors, communities, and society in general. Indeed, in its role as a trusted knowledge institution built on the foundation of a code of ethics, the museum has a greater responsibility to prioritize action than many other sectors. Just as more and more governments[16] are confirming that 2030 Agenda is the political frame for their work nationally and internationally, and the main political approach for addressing the greatest national and global challenges of our time, ICOM should embrace the same imperative and place Agenda 2030 at the heart of its activities in the decade ahead.

How, then, is ICOM to navigate its path through this increasingly demanding landscape, and what does it entail to place the resolution "On Sustainability and Implementing Agenda 2030" at the heart of its activities? At the halfway stage in the WGS's second mandate period, one can point to a series of initiatives taken by the group and the ICOM leadership. These initiatives follow the two pathways mentioned earlier: how ICOM can become sustainable in its operations; and how museums, through dissemination strategies and cross-sector cooperation, can assist their publics in attaining a sustainable future.

Among the former, we find a positive dialogue on the museum definition with DEFINE and the revision of the Code of Ethics with ETHCOM, and with the international and national committee spokespersons and several individual committees. The WGS is in the early stage of developing a channel for Indigenous voices on the question of sustainable futures and are advisers to Prague 2022 and an international conference on museums and sustainability to be held in Shanghai in November in collaboration with the International Museum Research and Exchange Centre at Shanghai University. The conference will also feature a sustainability webinar—one of a series of six regional webinars the working group is holding in the run-up to Prague. Another will be devoted to the sustainable approach to the reconstruction of the national museum of Brazil, Rio de Janeiro's Museu Nacional.

The WGS is also in the process of developing the idea of a sustainability ambassador program, which aims to broaden the base for action in implementing the Kyoto resolution at all levels of ICOM. All ICOM committees will be invited to nominate an ambassador, responsible for ensuring that each embraces Agenda 2030 in its activities and establishing a direct link between its members and the ICOM sustainability hub. It is important to emphasize that both individual members and a number of national and international committees have already engaged extensively with sustainability themes, independent of the working group. Indeed, we are seeing the start of a growing grassroots commitment for sustainable futures throughout ICOM and the museum sector.

Through its cross-sector enterprises, the working group has represented ICOM in EU sustainability initiatives, assisted the leadership in connection with ICOM's presence at PRE-COP[17] and COP26, and became an official supporter of the Global Coalition, United for Biodiversity. The group and its members have cooperated with university research departments on initiatives such as the Curating Climate Collaboratory at the Oslo School of Environmental Humanities and worked closely with other international museum organizations—the American Alliance of Museums (AAM), the Network of European Museum Organizations (NEMO), and We Are Museums—on initiatives highlighting the role of Agenda 2030. Other notable programs include ICOM president Alberto Garlandini's speech at a recent G20 meeting[18] and cross-sector collaboration with, among others, the International Centre for the Study of the Preservation and Restoration of Cultural Property (ICROM), the International Council on Monuments and Sites (ICOMOS), and the International Federation of Libraries and Institutions (IFLA).

However, despite these successes, when considering the implementation of the Kyoto resolution within the organization, the WGS has observed that the resolution, despite being the fulcrum of ICOM's approach, has yet to be implemented widely, suggesting perhaps a lack of awareness of the possibilities inherent in the agenda's holistic approach to sustainability's three spheres: the social, economic, and environmental, and culture's important role in achieving them.

Nonetheless, the adoption of the resolution and the choice of sustainability as a theme for Prague 2022 suggest a consensus within ICOM that asserts that museums have a significant role in assisting the global society in attaining the goals of Agenda 2030—one that takes its inspiration from the developing undergrowth of activism flourishing in the museum sector addressing these goals, and by tapping into the energy and commitment to be found in the growing size of citizens' movements demanding action led by the global youth movements and indigenous voices. As Bill McKibben writes, this is "particularly since August 2018 when Greta Thunberg began her first climate strike. There are thousands of Thunbergs now, scattered across the planet with millions of followers: this may be the biggest international movement in human history."[19]

ICOM has a duty to this public, especially the younger generation, to ensure that the museum family manifests a significant collective impact by activating the whole of its global organization and membership in addressing the goals of Agenda 2030 and its clarion call: Leave no one behind. As such, it is of utmost importance that the processes of developing a new museum definition, a possible revision of the ICOM code of ethics, together with ICOM's strategic plan for the decade in front of us, are imbued with the message found in the resolution from Kyoto. While acknowledging that different knowledge practices and worldviews invite disparate emphases in addressing Agenda 2030, there is much to commend the view that it should be foundational for the three processes. Moreover, embracing the ethical imperative that resonates through Agenda 2030 offers ICOM a means of augmenting the relationship between a new museum definition and ICOM's code of ethics. It also provides a framework to develop substantive strategic goals for ICOM in the decade leading up to 2030.

In the preface to her book *Braiding Sweetgrass*, Robin Wall Kimmerer, a mother, scientist, decorated professor, and member of the Citizen Potawatomi Nation, uses the metaphor of braiding to illuminate her goal of offering a series of stories meant to heal our relationship with the world. Perhaps ICOM, too, should consider creating a metaphorical braid—a four-strand braid, woven from the new museum definition, the revised code of ethics, the organization's strategic plans for the next decade, around the core of Agenda 2030. A strong braid would offer a means of empowerment for museum practitioners, the institution itself, and the people we serve. Kimmerer concludes her introduction by writing that her braid is "an intertwining of science, spirit and story—old stories and new ones that can be medicine for our broken relationship with the earth, a pharmacopoeia of healing stories that allow us to imagine a different relationship, in which people and land are good medicine for each other."

A sentiment resonating with optimism for the future, one that could easily be assimilated within the vision of the museum institution found in the Kyoto resolution on sustainability, is of "Empowering ourselves, our visitors and our communities through making positive contributions . . . in Transforming Our World."[20] It is a sentiment offering encouragement in the challenging tasks already facing us all.

A growing chorus of voices—McKibben's *biggest international movement in human history*—is demanding a system change. Moreover, as Wall Kimmerer suggests, we need new stories, a new narrative to replace the existing one that equates progress with the growth imperative that has been in place over the past seventy-five years and is at the heart of the crises facing the planet—a narrative that has measured progress in unlimited material growth through the means of Gross Domestic Product or GDP; one that maintains that as long as the economy continues to expand, we feel assured that life is getting better; we believe we are progressing, not just as individuals but also as societies.

A new narrative to replace the growth paradigm resonates with the findings of a recent global survey, which found that 74 percent of the population of the world's G20 nations believe humanity is pushing the planet toward a dangerous tipping point and support a shift of priorities away from economic profit.[21] This echoes the words of Robert Kennedy, who, as long ago as 1968, said:

> Yet the Gross National Product does not allow for the health of our children, the quality of their education or the joy of their play. It does not include the beauty of our poetry or the strength of our marriages, the intelligence of our public debate or the integrity of our public officials. It measures neither our wit or our courage, neither our wisdom nor our learning, neither our compassion nor our devotion to our country, it measures everything in short, except that which makes life worthwhile.[22]

Museums, as stewards of the global memory, are uniquely placed to contribute to the creation of a new narrative on such a shift of priorities, away from growth and toward sustainable futures. With its global network, ICOM is ideally placed to facilitate the telling of such a narrative. The IPCC AR6 final report is to be published in September 2022.[23] This might be a suitable place to begin developing such a new narrative. In cooperation with the IPCC, museums could be transformed into arenas for debate and dissemination in cooperation with local communities—a vision of museums as agents for change, enhancing public awareness, inspiring public action, and contributing to the goal of achieving a sustainable future through implementing an agenda to transform our world.

NOTES

1. Aliya Uteuova, "What Sea Level Rise Will Do to Famous American Sites, Visualized," *The Guardian*, October 12, 2021, https://www.theguardian.com/us-news/2021/oct/12/sea-level-rise-well-known-american-sites-visualized.
2. IPCC, *Climate Change 2021: The Physical Science Basis. Contribution of Working Group I to the Sixth Assessment Report of the Intergovernmental Panel on Climate Change* (Cambridge: Cambridge University Press, 2021), https://www.ipcc.ch/report/ar6/wg1/.
3. "IPCC Report: 'Code Red' for Human Driven Global Heating, Warns UN Chief," UN News, August 9, 2021, https://news.un.org/en/story/2021/08/1097362.
4. Rob Davies, "Carbon Emissions 'Will Drop Just 40% by 2050 with Countries' Current Pledges,'" *The Guardian*, October 13, 2021, https://www.theguardian.com/environment/2021/oct/13/carbon-emissions-will-drop-just-40-by-2050-with-countries-current-pledges.
5. "Living Planet Report 2020: Bending the Curve of Biodiversity Loss," WWF (2020), https://www.wwf.org.uk/sites/default/files/2020-09/LPR20_Full_report.pdf.
6. "Pathway to Critical and Formidable Goal of Net-Zero Emissions by 2050 Is Narrow but Brings Huge Benefits, According to IEA Special Report," IEA press release, May 18, 2021, https://www.iea.org/news/pathway-to-critical-and-formidable-goal-of-net-zero-emissions-by-2050-is-narrow-but-brings-huge-benefits.

7. "Adapt or Die, Says Environmental Agency," Environmental Agency, October 13, 2021, https://www.gov.uk/government/news/adapt-or-die-says-environment-agency.

8. Our Demands, Fridays for Future, https://fridaysforfuture.org/what-we-do/our-demands/.

9. https://sustainabledevelopment.un.org/content/documents/21252030%20Agenda%20for%20Sustainable%20Development%20web.pdf.

10. United Nations, Department of Economic and Social Affairs, Sustainable Development, "Transforming Our World: The 2030 Agenda for Sustainable Development," https://sdgs.un.org/2030agenda.

11. "On Sustainability and the Implementation of *Agenda 2030, Transforming Our World*," ICOM, https://icom.museum/wp-content/uploads/2021/01/Resolution-sustainability-EN-2.pdf.

12. "Museums and the Sustainable Development Goals," http://www.curatingtomorrow.co.uk/wp-content/uploads/2020/01/museums-and-the-sustainable-development-goals-2019.pdf.

13. "Report of the World Commission on Environment and Development: Our Common Future," https://sustainabledevelopment.un.org/content/documents/5987our-common-future.pdf.

14. "Working Group on Sustainability: Mandate 2020–2022," ICOM, https://icom.museum/wp-content/uploads/2020/12/WGS-Mandate-2020-2022.pdf.

15. Vaccine Equity, World Health Organization, https://www.who.int/campaigns/vaccine-equity.

16. Voluntary National Review 2021 Norway, https://www.regjeringen.no/no/dokumenter/voluntary-national-review/id2863155/?q=Agenda%202030.

17. ICOM Instagram post, September 23, 2021, https://www.instagram.com/p/CUKm_4aosKG/.

18. "The G20 Recognised the Key Role of Museums as Key Partners in Driving Sustainable Development and Fighting Climate Change," ICOM, https://icom.museum/en/news/the-g20-recognises-the-role-of-museums-and-icom-in-addressing-the-climate-crisis/.

19. Bill McKibben, "It's Easy to Feel Pessimistic about the Climate. But We've Got Two Big Things on Our Side," *The Guardian*, October 15, 2021, https://www.theguardian.com/commentisfree/2021/oct/15/climate-crisis-cop26-bill-mckibben.

20. "On Sustainability and the Implementation," ICOM.

21. Sophie Thompson and Bridget Williams, "Global Commons Survey: Attitudes to Transformation and Planetary Stewardship," Ipsos MORI, https://www.ipsos.com/ipsos-mori/en-uk/global-commons-survey-attitudes-transformation-and-planetary-stewardship.

22. Robert F. Kennedy, "Remarks at the University of Kansas, March 18, 1968," John F. Kennedy Presidential Library, MR 89–34, Miscellaneous Recordings, https://www.jfklibrary.org/learn/about-jfk/the-kennedy-family/robert-f-kennedy/robert-f-kennedy-speeches/remarks-at-the-university-of-kansas-march-18-1968.

23. "AR6 Synthesis Report," IPCC, https://www.ipcc.ch/report/sixth-assessment-report-cycle/.

24

The Museum's Role in the Global Effort to Create a World Where Everyone and Everything Can Thrive

Sarah Sutton

Museums are extraordinarily well suited to resolve issues and recognize responsibilities associated with environmental sustainability. Museums' domains of expertise embrace all that is critical in pursuing the kind of sustainability that enables everyone and everything to thrive:

1. study, research, and education;
2. public enrichment and engagement; and
3. stewardship and protection of cultural and scientific knowledge and resources.

In at *least* these three areas, museum professionals are continually improving their practice in ways that respond to both the needs of the world around museums and to the pressures of that world on museum work. That continuous improvement is critical: the pace of climate change is so great as to overwhelm the hard efforts of a year in a terrifying moment and to wipe out centuries of culture just as quickly.

MUSEUMS, AGENDA 2030, AND THE UNITED NATIONS' SUSTAINABLE DEVELOPMENT GOALS

In 2019, when the International Council of Museums (ICOM) membership committed itself to pursuing Agenda 2030 as a guide for the next three years, it embraced a road map to sustainability. Agenda 2030 was created through an agreement by 193 global heads of state in 2015, three months before the historic Paris Agreement was confirmed. Agenda 2030 is based on the seventeen Sustainable Development Goals, or SDGs, which have specific actions and targets that, if achieved, can lead us to global change that protects the planet and creates a world where people are free from poverty, hunger, fear, and discrimination in ways that ensure peace and individual prosperity, all of it developed through partnerships that create new solutions and approaches that benefit everyone together.[1] Though the SDGs and Agenda 2030 may appear removed from the general public and from our daily work, perhaps as goals only attainable through policy and international cooperation, that is decidedly not the case. They are where museums have an important role in sustainability.

Agenda 2030 focuses our work, and everyone else's as well, on limiting the average warming of the Earth to 1.5° C to avoid the worst impacts of climate change. Everyone must participate in the change effort—every family, individual, organization, corporation, and policy maker; every artist, fisher person, and museum worker. Nothing short of a whole-of-society approach is sufficient, according to abundant current scientific data. Agenda 2030 and the SDGs are that path for museums to participate. Museum professional and author Henry McGhie describes museums' relationships to the SDGs this way:

> The SDGs are not just for governments: they are an invitation to all sectors of society, in all places, to collaborate and participate in the achievement of the 2030 Agenda. The SDGs are an incredible opportunity for anyone, any organisation, and any sector to collaborate in pursuit of common goals, levering their skills, capacities and unique resources. Museums have a great deal to offer this Agenda, and some of the SDGs will not be achieved without museums. . . . The SDGs are . . . not about continuing with business as usual, but about clear, committed, focused action to enhance positive impacts and reduce negative impacts.[2]

The IIC, ICCROM, and ICOM-CC Joint Commitment for Climate Action in Cultural Heritage is a powerful example of how the sector leadership can help all museum workers recognize and pursue this new level of performance:

> The signatories not only commit to tackling carbon emissions and achieving net zero within their own organisations, but also to promoting our collective ambition to align with the UN 2030 Agenda for sustainable development. Kate Seymour, the chair of ICOM-CC when the pact was made, recognized the value of museum workers and the profession in sustainability work and climate action, stating that "Individual choices will have an impact, *especially* if we do them as a community."[3]

MEASURING SUSTAINABILITY IMPACTS

The SDGs have targets with metrics that help any entity, including museums, measure sustainability. Museums can measure languages saved, girls given new opportunities, species protected, carbon footprints and carbon avoided or sequestered, energy generated, or people lifted out of poverty. Each of these is a measurable impact that museums can register. Museum workers are well versed in planning research, programs, and exhibits in both short and long time frames, and in setting goals and measuring impacts, just as we are asked to do with the SDGs. They are a plan-with-impacts approach for securing a lasting future for all that we care for on this planet.

Every five years, each signatory to the Paris Agreement submits its Nationally Determined Contribution (NDC) to ensuring the success of the Paris Agreement. Each nation makes its own choices but should create these NDCs in a manner that supports all seventeen of the SDGs and makes progress against the targets. Though, again, this seems the domain of governments, success in reaching those targets requires everyone's actions, and museums can contribute significantly. Each of the measurable impacts identified earlier can be added to a nation's NDC, registering not only a nation's progress toward its own goals, but also the value of museums in doing that work. The irony is that, if we do not pursue sustainability, then all of our stewardship efforts are wasted. Only in a safe world, filled with people free from want and fear, will we be able to invest—physically and morally— in the stewardship of the centuries of materials and knowledge we've cared for in our profession.

MUSEUMS AS INCUBATORS FOR SOCIAL AND ENVIRONMENTAL WELL-BEING AND CHANGE

Doing sustainability work requires some practice and some specific information (most often acquired through partners and rarely part of our innate knowledge). Repeatedly, we see how it is entirely achievable by anyone who is curious, courageous, and committed enough to try, especially museum workers able to call upon the resources of the institution: "Museums hold in one body the diverse physical and intellectual resources, abilities, creativity, freedom, and authority to foster the changes the world needs most."[4] Museums have *all* the necessary components for successfully tackling the most challenging issues:

- collections
- curators, registrars, conservators, collections managers, and researchers
- educators and exhibit designers
- facilities operators and landscape managers
- fund-raisers, media managers, and administrators
- partners, community members, and visitors

These components empower museums to develop their domains of expertise and responsibility—noted earlier as 1) study, research, and education; 2) public enrichment and engagement; and 3) stewardship and protection of cultural and scientific knowledge and resources—and to participate in local, regional, national, and global efforts to build that world where everyone and everything can thrive. As we work to create that safe world, if we follow the sustainable development approach, we will protect that which we care for and care about, and have the joy and opportunity of adding to the cultural and natural record in valuable ways for all—and can count on a future with thriving cultures here to value it, too. The secretary of the Smithsonian, Lonnie G. Bunch III, has written about the culture and heritage sector's responsibility to address climate change. His words apply equally to all museums:

> Our environmental crisis is complex and far-reaching. The constellation of different challenges it brings together—biodiversity, economics, politics, culture—it affects us all. Addressing an interdisciplinary challenge requires an interdisciplinary approach. . . . We have an opportunity to harness the full strength of our research, programs, education, and convening capacity. This is an opportunity to advance groundbreaking research. To weave sustainable practices into every aspect of our operations. To bring together different constituencies and tell the stories that need to be heard.[5]

This complexity, this interdisciplinarity, is exactly what calls a museum to engage in sustainability. National leaders do not have the capacity to satisfy Agenda 2030 without a whole-of-society approach. Museums and their cultural and community partners can speak for culture and heritage, for advancing knowledge in culture and science, and for sharing that knowledge with anyone interested in learning. No other portion of society can fulfill these specific responsibilities sufficiently. Conversely, a museum cannot satisfy all the SDGs. It can, however, continually prioritize those that align with its evolving mission while supporting and nurturing its community or communities. This is the only way that the museum can sustain its relevance and value to society, the only way it can secure its future.

SUSTAINABILITY'S LESSONS FOR SOLVING WICKED PROBLEMS

Some in the museum sector still resist sustainability actions. They may claim lack of time and material resources for an "additional" responsibility. Others claim not to have the money to tackle this change, or the social license to focus on it. They cite competing claims for their time on issues of social justice, financial survival, and professional commitments requiring their attention. Nonsense. The SDGs clearly demonstrate how sustainability aligns with social justice and with institutional prosperity, and the health and safety of the *ultimate* collections storage and exhibition space—the planet. Nowhere do the SDGs ask a professional to compromise principles or expertise. Instead, the principles of sustainability ask that a professional examine purpose and responsibility, and then gather the most effective resources for a positive result.

Indeed, this *does* require updating the practices of museum workers now and into the future as the world continues to evolve socially, financially, and environmentally. Every other issue of social change has required the same of the profession whether or not museum workers complied. The sector has struggled with colonialism, theft and forgery, elitism, and power and subjugation. It has adapted to new financial regulations, and accessibility responsibilities and regulations. Each country continues to cobble together its distinct funding mechanisms for museums—and never, ever enough of it.

This change requires systems thinking, including choices about where to influence, disturb, or disrupt the current systems museums use to do their work through collections management, research, public engagement, operations, and governance. These systems can be influenced positively through training, funding, and dissemination of new research and practices. They can also be disrupted enough to create change through the requirement of new policies or practices, such as carbon footprints, climate action plans, and energy efficiency policies. They can also be disrupted entirely by influences similar to the COVID-19 pandemic, when barriers to staff travel accelerated the use of tools strengthening the confidence in bookend and virtual couriers rather than human couriers. When mere influence and encouragement do not create enough change, disruption and disturbances can and will. Museum workers can change by choice rather than force.

The sector has continuously improved its professional practice as it has matured. It should always do so. As every aspect of this profession is reevaluated for its positive and negative effects on the planet and its people, museum workers will share with each other what they discover. They will raise each other up in this work as they improve professional practice. That critical, creative, generous thinking is what museums have always been called upon to nurture. Museums and their workers must care for the planet and for each other, or who, in this story, can possibly come along behind us to take up these duties we hold so dear?

NOTES

1. United Nations, Department of Economic and Social Affairs, Sustainable Development, "Transforming Our World: The 2030 Agenda for Sustainable Development," https://sdgs.un.org/2030agenda.
2. "Museums and the Sustainable Development Goals," http://www.curatingtomorrow .co.uk/wp-content/uploads/2020/01/museums-and-the-sustainable-develop ment-goals-2019.pdf, 8.
3. "Joint Commitment on Climate Action for Cultural Heritage," https://www.iicon servation.org/content/iic-iccrom-and-icom-cc-agree-joint-commitment-climate -action-cultural-heritage.

4. Sarah W. Sutton, Elizabeth Wylie, Beka Economopoulos, Carter O'Brien, Stephanie Shapiro, and Shengyin Xu, "Museums and the Future of a Healthy World: 'Just, Verdant and Peaceful,'" *Curator: The Museum Journal* 60, no. 2 (2017): 151.

5. Rebecca Rushfield, ed., *Stemming the Tide: Global Strategies for Sustaining Cultural Heritage through Climate Change* (Washington, DC: Smithsonian Scholarly Press, 2021), iv.

Part Seven

What Now/
Now What?

25

Seizing the Moment

THE EVOLUTION OF THE TWENTY-FIRST-CENTURY MUSEUM

Lonnie G. Bunch III

When the ICOM-US Museum Definition Task Force began discussing how to define a museum, it was an attempt to answer the fundamental questions of the twenty-first century for our institutions: How can we best be of value, and how can we be places that respect our history without being held captive by that past? Today, a clarion call is to build on our most valued traditions to reimagine and reinvent our cultural institutions. We must seize the opportunity in front of us to be institutions that matter both in traditional ways and in ways that have a more contemporary resonance.

It was clear to me when this project began that cultural institutions must change to survive. We cannot pretend to be above the fray when it comes to issues that matter most to the communities we serve. We must address them head-on when we think about what museums are and what we should be. That does not mean that we should jettison all museum traditions, nor should we ignore the audiences we have cultivated in the past. But we must not allow our traditions to trap us in the past like fossils in amber. Fear of change can prevent innovation and creativity. As society, technology, and expectations change, we must change with them if we are to remain relevant.

The urgency of that need intensified during the past year and a half, as the world has grappled with what I call the dual pandemics of COVID-19 and systemic racism. The time line for action has been moved up; we no longer have the luxury of treating the redefinition of museums as an academic question. It is an existential one.

THE IMPACT OF A DEADLY PANDEMIC

When COVID-19 hit, the scope of the disaster was hard to comprehend. It has been a traumatic experience for people unlike any most of us have seen. The grief and emotional turmoil caused by loss of life, long-term effects, and worry for our loved ones have been overwhelming. And the economic impact has been devastating. The issues ICOM-US began discussing in 2019 were underscored emphatically.

The museum community has been hit especially hard by the economic fallout of COVID-19. The statistics are daunting: 90 percent of museums around the world have had to close. As many as 13 percent of them might be unable to reopen.[1] In April 2021, UNESCO updated its report on the state of museums during the pandemic. It estimated that revenues on average have fallen 80 percent at cultural institutions since 2019.[2]

That is clearly unsustainable. As we have discussions to decide what museums are and should be, I think we must seriously consider sustainability—not only in the environmental sense, but also in terms of the long-term viability of our organizations.

As we face hard fiscal choices and loss of revenue at our museums, it would be easy to retreat to caution, to wait until we are on firmer ground to take risks or innovate. I urge the exact opposite. In this time of turmoil and uncertainty, we cannot afford *not* to take risks, innovate, and think differently about our mission. This is a moment of great pain but also of great possibility. And we need to set our sights beyond survival.

We have a radical opportunity here—not just to recover the revenue we have lost, but to reimagine the exciting possibilities, reconnect with our audiences in new ways, and revitalize the ways we serve our communities and nations. If we can do that, I am confident that we can emerge from this crisis as a unified museum field, strengthened by the challenges we have overcome and improved by the wisdom we have gained.

MUSEUMS' ROLE IN SOCIAL JUSTICE

Although COVID-19 has been a primary concern for museums, ongoing racial and social injustice has also forced cultural institutions to rethink what we stand for and how we should respond. The worldwide protests over the killing of George Floyd and the wider problem of police brutality aimed at communities of color left so many institutions with a sense of obligation to respond.

I have been so impressed by the way cultural institutions have used this moment to try to bridge our racial and cultural differences by being places that seek to foster understanding and conversation about race, gender, and identity. One example of how art can do this is found in Sacramento's Crocker Art Museum. Its *Legends from Los Angeles* exhibition is a brilliant exploration of African American life and a powerful refutation of gender and racial stereotypes, seen through the lenses of gifted artists Betye Saar and her two daughters, Lezley and Alison Saar.[3]

The contemporary art exhibition at Northwestern University's Block Museum of Art, *Who Says, Who Shows, What Counts*, challenges museums to think about the White, mainstream narratives normally elevated in their collections. The exhibition is also an exercise in democratizing the process: the curators gave the artists, mostly people of color, the opportunity to take the lead in choosing the content. And instead of labeling the artworks as curators typically do, they also asked Northwestern students, alumni, faculty, and staff to do so.[4]

At the Smithsonian, our Asian Pacific American Center collected more than 260 different resources for teachers and the public to address stereotypes and bias that the Asian American Pacific Islander community has faced.

And one of the Smithsonian-wide initiatives aiming to make an impact is *Our Shared Future: Reckoning with Our Racial Past*. By conducting virtual and live events with diverse audiences from all parts of the country, we hope to better understand how different people experience race, leading to a more robust national conversation to help bridge our racial divide. Digital content and learning resources will give students and educators the tools to experience a fuller, more accurate picture of the nation's complex history.

MUSEUMS AS PLACES OF HEALING AND REFLECTION

There has also been a widespread recognition by the museum community of the emotional and psychological toll COVID-19 and systemic racism have taken on the nation. Many are using this time to document what people are going through, not just so we can help our audiences and employees navigate the difficulties, but so we can help people in future generations understand this moment.

For example, the California Historical Society has reached out to its visitors to answer questions about the coronavirus and to send pictures that represent their experiences. Our Anacostia Community Museum has also curated inspiring stories about how people are supporting one another during these pandemics on its Moments of Resilience website. And the Smithsonian went to the front lines of history as it happened last year, deploying rapid-response collecting teams to acquire materials related to the first-known doses of the COVID-19 vaccine, items from the George Floyd protests, and objects from the Capitol insurrection.

We should never minimize the impact these dual pandemics have had on our collective psyche. But the way so many have responded shows that we have an unparalleled opportunity to reinvent ourselves. This is the moment to reimagine our institutions, our relationships with our audiences, our business models, and the way we serve our communities and our countries.

MUSEUMS SHOW WHAT SERVICE LOOKS LIKE

One thing that museums have proven during this difficult time is our ability to make a difference in our communities in ways people do not normally connect with museums. For instance, as the pandemic worsened, hospitals experienced drastic shortages of personal protective equipment such as masks and gloves. Museums, galleries, and other arts institutions across the country, including the Metropolitan Museum of Art in New York, the San Francisco Museum of Modern Art, and the Chicago History Museum, donated the supplies they had to the nurses, doctors, and other medical staff who needed it most.

As businesses closed and unemployment soared during the height of the pandemic, food insecurity grew more pronounced. According to the United Nations, as many as 161 million more people faced hunger in 2020 than in 2019.[5] The Smithsonian's Anacostia Community Museum is working to combat that. Its exhibition *Food for the People* illuminates food insecurity in the Washington, D.C., metropolitan area. The museum pairs that traditional educational component with real action, working with Feed the Fridge, a program that places stocked refrigerators, free for all to use, into areas with high levels of food insecurity. The fridge in the museum's parking lot has provided five hundred free meals a week since January 2021 and will operate throughout 2022.

In San Bernardino County, California, the staff of the San Bernardino County Museum, like other California public employees, are required to serve as disaster service workers during an emergency. When the pandemic struck and the building closed to the public, many of the museum's employees were temporarily reassigned, working as contact tracers, helping at the local medical center, and pitching in as poll workers and drivers when there was a shortage of available people during the November 2020 election.[6]

The Museum of Contemporary Art Detroit (MOCAD) recognized the impact COVID-19 was having on the region's artists, so it partnered with the City of Detroit Office of Arts, Culture and Entrepreneurship to create the Rapid Response Fundraiser for Artists and Creatives. The online fund-raiser sold local art on MOCAD's website, with the artists and the museum splitting the profits 50/50.[7]

None of these falls into the category of traditional museum functions, but they show the potential for us all to serve our communities in a direct and profound way.

MUSEUMS APPLY SCIENCE TO OUR BIGGEST PROBLEMS

Museum professionals stepped up in myriad ways to help the people we serve during this moment. One way is through the often-underappreciated role as vital repositories of science-based research and education. As the coronavirus disease has made a profound impact throughout the world, the scientific insights our institutions have provided are invaluable in giving people the tools to understand, cope with, and protect themselves from COVID-19.

Many institutions have created exhibitions that educate people on COVID-19, including the Space Center Houston, the New York Hall of Science, and the National Museum of Emerging Science and Innovation (Miraikan) in Tokyo.[8] At the Smithsonian's National Museum of Natural History, *Outbreak: Epidemics in a Connected World* allows visitors to participate in an interactive simulation to find connections among human, animal, and environmental health; play a cooperative game in which they try to control an outbreak; and experience the firsthand accounts of disease survivors and health-care workers.

Other institutions, such as the Pacific Science Center in Seattle, and the Smithsonian created websites that collated the latest coronavirus disease research, public health guidance, and information about the pandemic's impact.

And the veterinarians and researchers of the Smithsonian Conservation Biology Institute's Global Health Program have worked with USAID to identify dangerous zoonotic diseases before they become pandemic threats and to expedite a rapid response to currently undetected viruses. In May 2021, scientists from across the Smithsonian's many scientific units and our partners released a plan for a new, multifaceted approach to modeling infectious diseases, applying existing methods for studying the planet's natural systems to disease-causing pathogens. Given the amount of global coordination, massive data, and investment needed for this kind of systems-level, collaborative approach to forecasting disease emergence, the challenges would be significant. But the benefits could be immense, with the process applicable to other areas of study such as economics.[9]

USING DIGITAL TECHNOLOGY TO CARRY OUT OUR MISSIONS

Museum professionals have also proven agile when it comes to finding new ways of creating and sharing exhibitions, programming, and curricula. I have been inspired and impressed by the work of Smithsonian curators, educators, scientists, and scholars who rose to the challenge, especially in using technology to reach audiences in creative new ways.

For instance, the Smithsonian Open Access collection, more than 3 million free digital items from the Institution's collections, has been viewed more than 25 million times and downloaded nearly 800,000 times in the past three months alone. The Cooper Hewitt, Smithsonian Design Museum, in New York, solicited and funded prototypes for digital platforms based on our Open Access objects. The ideas that people had were fascinating, including a Web-based virtual reality portal that lets audiences navigate a museum using sound and an educational video game that asks players to work collaboratively to discover, collect, and authenticate artifacts.

We have countless other examples of cultural institutions across the country and around the world embracing technology to reach their audiences.

The Guggenheim collaborated with the *99% Invisible* podcast to explore the museum's unseen architecture and history, producing an onsite audio tour and a multilingual podcast for listeners.[10]

The program Create Together at Crystal Bridges Museum of American Art in Bentonville, Arkansas, uses the oil paintings in its collections as online lessons that inspire people of all ages to make their own art and post it on social media. Videos by the museum's educators help guide participants through the process and teach them about the oil paintings they see.

One wholly unexpected but wildly successful instance of a museum using the internet to reach new audiences has been the Sacramento History Museum's embrace of social media. This traditional museum focuses on the history of California's capital and the Gold Rush, but its outreach has proven to be anything but traditional.

While closed to the public, the museum decided to start a TikTok account, with one of the videos featuring an eighty-two-year-old volunteer demonstrating a nineteenth-century printing press in the collection. The video went viral, causing people to follow the account and generating much buzz for the museum among a much-coveted young demographic. As of September 2021, the Sacramento History Museum has nearly 2 million TikTok followers worldwide, more than any other museum in the world, and its posts have been liked more than 23 million times.[11] It is an example of how cultural institutions can benefit from daring to be unconventional.

So, what lessons have museums learned from this moment that we can apply in the decades ahead to ensure that we not only survive but thrive?

RETHINKING THE PHYSICAL SPACE OF THE MUSEUM

Even as museums reopen, a significant percentage of people who visited before will be reluctant to return in person. These people are still our audiences. Cultural institutions will have to continue to focus on bringing the museum experiences to everyone, no matter where they are and no matter their preferred platform for accessing our programming and exhibitions.

We will also have to rethink the buildings themselves. We know they will need to change, not just to deal with COVID-19, but in anticipation of the next pandemic or to become more resilient to environmental factors such as climate change or earthquakes. We can look to history for examples of museum design that has adapted in the face of external challenges.

When the Broad Museum in Los Angeles was built in 2015, it was designed to withstand earthquakes. When Superstorm Sandy hit New York in October 2012, as the new Whitney Museum of American Art was being built, it caused its planners to change the design, raising the elevation and incorporating waterproof materials, a flood door, and a mobile wall that can protect the museum from storm surge.[12]

Aside from building new museums that allow for freer movement, have robust ventilation that incorporates natural airflow, and integrate materials that are resistant to germs and bacteria, it is also clear that we will need to be less reliant on physical spaces and more open to the technology that allows us to reach people where they are.

When our buildings closed, online resources became our primary mode of connection. And even as restrictions on in-person visits were gradually lifted, we saw that the public was increasingly eager to consume content digitally, but only if it met the high standards expected of us.

Collections will always be the foundation of museum scholarship, science, exhibitions, and education. But the reality is that millions of people will never be able to visit our museums because of logistics or cost. Given ubiquitous modern technology, though, so many can visit us from their laptops and cell phones, whether in schools or at home.

Embracing the digital experience does not mean abandoning the traditional strengths of our organizations. As a historian, I appreciate that there is no substitute for seeing the real thing, be it an iconic artifact that encapsulates a turning point in history or a priceless work of art that stirs the soul.

That is why I do not suggest we should think about online platforms as replacements for our in-person offerings. To the contrary, digital museum experiences are complementary, offering their own strengths that are fundamentally different from in-person visits.

We also know that not everyone has equal access to modern technology, one unfortunate example of how low-income communities and communities of color have disproportionately borne the effects of the pandemic. That is why, in addition to bringing our vast resources to bear on digital platforms, it is equally important to create educational programming that does not rely on a laptop or a smartphone.

During the pandemic, educators from across the Smithsonian began collaborating with *USA Today*. They are producing a series of low-tech educational materials based on our museum collections and activities. Since June 2020, we have distributed 545,000 print activity guides for children and 3.7 million printed newspaper inserts for intergenerational learning.

REVITALIZING AND REINFORCING MUSEUMS' EDUCATIONAL MISSIONS WITH MEANINGFUL DIALOGUE

As the son of educators, I believe museums have an enormous responsibility in providing support to formal education systems. I look to the Smithsonian's partnership with the Washington, D.C., public school system as a model for how all museums can and must engage classrooms across the country.

We must all work to do more to offer resources that enhance classroom learning, provide professional development for teachers, and cultivate deeper connections with educators and students in our communities.

Another aspect of the modern museum is whether it is realistic to think that we can be agents of change without appearing to be political. Taking into consideration social and racial disparities is not inherently political when determining content. It is, however, necessary if cultural institutions want to maximize impact and expand our audiences.

For museums to thrive, we will need to be more than repositories of historic information or artifacts. We will also need to become engaged in contemporary issues that matter to people by leading honest, constructive dialogue. Museums do not need to be activist organizations, but we must address contemporary issues that are important to the audiences we serve, or we risk becoming out of touch, antiquated, and irrelevant.

DIVERSIFYING OUR AUDIENCES AND WORKFORCE

Cultural institutions looking to remain relevant must also creatively engage people who have historically been overlooked by museums. It is no longer enough to rely on the old ways of doing things: museums can and must do more to embrace new, diverse, multigenerational audiences.

Focusing on diversity, equity, accessibility, and inclusiveness when thinking about programming, exhibitions, educational content, and staffing does not mean to be politically correct, nor does it need to be political. It is, however, doing the right thing and the smart thing. By responding to changing societal norms, we better serve our mission and our communities, and we ensure that museums do not go the way of the dinosaurs displayed in our halls. Museums do not have the luxury of prizing exclusivity over access.

When I was helping to bring the National Museum of African American History and Culture to life, there was concern over what our visitation would look like. And I am incredibly proud to say that since its opening, the museum has attracted one of the most diverse audiences of any Smithsonian institution.

But I am even more proud that 30 percent of our visitors were first-time museumgoers. As we wonder about the long-term effects of COVID-19 and think about how we can ensure that visitors return to our museums, these numbers paint a clear picture. Complex, diverse, community-driven stories will increase interest in museums.

To me, this evidence suggests that it is possible for all of us to expand our bases. We hamstring ourselves by serving only a narrow slice of our populations. When we put in the effort to serve people who have not always been made to feel welcome at museums, it pays off in the long run.

Candidly, we cannot serve these audiences if we do not first hold ourselves accountable. We need to model the diversity of our public in our exhibitions, our research, our boardrooms, and our staff.

As someone who has spent his career challenging museums to be more diverse and inclusive places, it is clear that we have made significant strides. But we also have further to go. Our profession will become stronger and more resilient during moments of crisis when we represent the full experiences of the public. To tell those stories, we need the perspective that a diverse, inclusive workforce can bring.

FINAL THOUGHTS

I believe museums of all kinds have the obligation to use our expertise and platforms for the greater good. We can and must reach more people, be more relevant to their lives, and have a more profound impact.

This is not a moment to do things as they have always been done, to retreat to familiarity. It is an opportunity to try a better way and to take inspiration from so many museums that have taken risks because they have had to, applying their creativity for the benefit of those they serve. I believe the successful museums in the years ahead will be those that embrace an entrepreneurial spirit, creating entirely new viewing and learning experiences.

The crises we have faced and adapted to have proven that museums can be more than community centers. We can be central to our communities.

We can uphold museum traditions while expanding our missions. We can strengthen our outreach to find new, more diverse audiences. And we can use the artistry, culture, science, scholarship, and education found in our museums to help our citizens, our communities, and our countries.

To be candid, none of these suggestions is groundbreaking. They are simply a reminder that museums can be breathtaking places that illuminate our shared humanity when we have the courage to dream big, no matter how daunting the challenge.

In 1991, at the height of the AIDS crisis, eight science museums were enlisted to be a part of the National AIDS Exhibition Consortium to create exhibitions that could educate the public about AIDS. But it became something much more profound when the museums' curators and educators opted to tell the poignant stories of people living with HIV and AIDS—people of all genders, races, and sexual orientations who are often overshadowed by the statistics.[13] That is the kind of inclusive, transformative, and life-affirming impact museums can make if we prioritize our shared future when considering how to serve our communities.

ICOM's project to define museums in a way that accurately reflects our modern ethical responsibilities as institutions is invaluable. By brainstorming, collaborating, and clarifying our long-term goals, we improve our ability to serve our audiences. Defining museums not based simply on what we have done in the past, but on what we have the potential to do in the future, is an exciting prospect.

The process itself has been educational, with some obstacles along the way, but ultimately it will make ICOM a stronger organization and the museum profession nimbler and more proactive. And I think this effort will end up being a model for how museums should work with communities: by soliciting input, showing transparency, and seeking consensus.

I look forward to being part of the discussions that will lead to a thoughtful, inclusive, and ambitious definition that reflects the work institutions across the country and around the world are doing to become more robust and resilient.

As ICOM explores the definition of what a museum is, I think that determining the answer to the question "What now?" is up to all of us. I have confidence that the museum community will find ways to work together more closely to chart a path to a vibrant, dynamic future for museums everywhere.

NOTES

1. Associated Press, "Ninety Percent of the World's Museums Were Closed by the Coronavirus Pandemic, and One in Eight May Never Reopen," May 19, 2020, https://www.marketwatch.com/story/ninety-percent-of-the-worlds-museums -were-closed-by-the-coronavirus-pandemic-and-one-in-eight-may-never-reopen -2020-05-19.
2. "Museums around the World: In the Face of COVID-19," UNESCO, https://unesdoc .unesco.org/ark:/48223/pf0000376729_eng/PDF/376729eng.pdf.multi.
3. See Letha Ch'ien, "Crocker Art Museum Celebrates Saar Family's Powerful Work Challenging Race and Gender Stereotypes," Datebook, April 16, 2021, https://date book.sfchronicle.com/art-exhibits/crocker-art-museum-celebrates-saar-familys -powerful-work-challenging-race-and-gender-stereotypes.
4. Marc Vitali, "New Exhibit at Block Museum Looks at Which Art Gets Shown and Why," WTTW, October 27, 2021, https://news.wttw.com/2021/10/27/new -exhibit-block-museum-looks-which-art-gets-shown-and-why; Alexa Crowder, "The Block Museum's Fall Exhibition, 'Who Says, Who Shows, What Counts' Questions Historical Narratives," *Daily Northwestern*, October 4, 2021, https:// dailynorthwestern.com/2021/10/04/ae/the-block-museums-fall-exhibition-who -shows-who-says-what-counts-questions-historical-narratives/.
5. "The State of Food Security and Nutrition in the World 2021: The World Is at a Critical Juncture," Food and Agriculture Organization of the United Nations, https:// www.fao.org/state-of-food-security-nutrition.
6. "Museum Staff as Disaster Service Workers," Center for the Future of Museums Blog, October 11, 2021, https://www.aam-us.org/2021/10/11/museum-staff-as-disaster -service-workers/.
7. Karen Dybis, "MOCAD Launches Fundraiser to Support Detroit," *Seen*, June 5, 2020, https://seenthemagazine.com/mocad-launches-fundraiser-to-support-detroit -artists/.
8. "Engaging the Public with the Science of Coronavirus," Association of Science and Technology Centers, https://www.astc.org/coronavirus/engaging-the-public -with-the-science-of-coronavirus/.
9. "New Model for Infectious Disease Could Better Predict Future Pandemics," PreventionWeb, May 18, 2021, https://www.preventionweb.net/news/new-model-infec tious-disease-could-better-predict-future-pandemics.

10. "How Museums Are Adapting Programming to Keep People Engaged during COVID-19," Eriksen Translations, https://eriksen.com/arts-culture/covid-19-pro gramming-museums/.
11. Manuel Charr, "Printing Press Attracts Millions to Sacramento History Museum's TikTok Account," Museum Next, https://www.museumnext.com/article/printing -press-attracts-millions-to-sacramento-history-museums-tiktok-account/.
12. "Museums Are Better Prepared Than Most Americans to Survive the Next Natural Disaster," Grist, October 27, 2017, https://grist.org/article/museums-are-better -prepared-than-most-americans-to-survive-the-next-natural-disaster/.
13. "Lessons from History: Museums and Pandemics," Center for the Future of Museums Blog, March 10, 2020, https://www.aam-us.org/2020/03/10/lessons -from-history-museums-and-pandemics/.

The United States National Committee of the International Council of Museums

The International Council of Museums (ICOM) is a nonprofit, nongovernmental organization, founded in 1946, dedicated to the improvement and advancement of the world's museums and the museum profession, as well as the preservation of cultural heritage. Headquartered in Paris, France, ICOM has consultative status with UNESCO and with other international organizations, such as the World Intellectual Property Organization, and is the only international organization made up of museums and museum professionals; ICOM is similar to the United Nations.

In every country in which it operates, ICOM serves museums and museum professionals through a "National Committee" that promotes and facilitates membership in ICOM and advocates for the international museum interests of each country and its perspectives within ICOM. In addition, ICOM sponsors more than thirty subject-specific international committees for museum professionals and more than two hundred professional gatherings each year. ICOM currently represents more than forty-four thousand members and museums worldwide.

The U.S. National Committee is called ICOM-US and has functioned most recently as an independent, nonprofit organization; ICOM-US is one of 122 National Committees and regional alliances of ICOM. ICOM-US currently has some fourteen hundred members, with a high participation rate in the subject-specific committees. Among its activities, ICOM-US cosponsors and hosts international conferences and meetings of the ICOM subject-specific committees.

MEMBERS EX-OFFICIO

Dr. Eric Dorfman, director and CEO, North Carolina Museum of Natural Sciences (member, ICOM Executive Board)

Diana Pardue, director, Museum Services Division, Statue of Liberty and Ellis Island Immigration Museum (chair, Disaster Risk Management Committee DRMC)

Antonio Rodriguez, museum consultant (chair, International Committee for Exhibitions and Exchange ICEE)

Ute Wartenberg, executive director, American Numismatic Society (chair, International Committee for Money and Banking Museums ICOMON)

Sally Yerkovich, professor, museum anthropology, Columbia University (member, International Committee for Ethics—ETHICS)

ICOM-US board of directors at the Penn Museum in 2019. *Courtesy of ICOM-US*

Index

global transformation, ix
global warming, 134-35, 137
governance, 9, 11, 39, 93, 155; goals, 12; model, 9, reform, 11
governing boards, 11, 39, 118
Greece: Ancient Greek, 77; sculptures, 69
greenhouse gas emissions, 132, 134,
Guerrilla Girls, 80
Gurian, Elaine Heumann, xiv, 3-6, 15-20, 46-48
Guterres, António, 143

Hamlin, Chauncey Jerome, ix, xv
harassment, 36
Harlem Renaissance, 69
Harmon, Charles, xv
Harriet Beecher Stowe Center, 38
health care, xiv, 84, 86
health crisis, 11. *See also* crisis
heritage, ix, x, 12, 22, 27, 43, 45, 48, 51-52, 61, 84-86, 89, 117, 132, 154; access to, x, xvi, 27; civil rights, 38; collections, 34; communication of, ix; conservation of, ix; cultural, 51, 88, 114, 154; democracy, 53, 61; destruction, 87; exhibition of, ix; environmental, 124; historic, 51; institutions, 59, 88; intangible, ix, 21, 51, 85-86, 88, 114; Irish, 38; natural, x; national, 53; organizations, xi; preservation, 113, 115; protection, xii; research of, ix; scientific, 54; sector, 154; tangible, ix, 21, 51, 85; Ukrainian, 44; world, 53
Hickok, Gene, 39
Hinz, Hans-Martin, 44
historic site, 35, 38-39
history, 4, 12, 24, 29, 31-33, 35, 38-39, 44, 47, 69, 84; art, 55, 66, 81-82, 94, 99, 140, 159, 161, 164; ancestral, 95; civil rights, 23, 38; collection, 82; cultural, 24; erased, 97; European Union, 45, 95; exhibitions, 96; of funding, 96; human, 147-48; of ICOM, xii, 114, 116; institutional, 96; museum, 45, 52, 80-81, 108-9; national, 18, 44; natural, 32, 34, 77, 80-81; power of, 35; preservation of, 139; of

public housing, 139-40; repetition of, 19; social, 127; South Africa, 39; Ukrainian, 44; United States, 21, 139; of violence, 138; Western European, 21; of Whiteness, 53, 97
Holabird, John, 138
Holocaust, 19
Homes, Jane Addams, 138
"How Do We Center People in Museums?" conference, 15-16
Honchar, Ivan, 44, 45
human(s), 16, 40, 53, 62, 67-68, 78, 85, 87, 114, 135, 143, 145, 163; accomplishment, 52; behavior, 85; capital, 108; compassion, 17, 110; couriers, 155; creativity, 12; dignity, xvi, 100; experience, 24, 111; expression, 12; history, 107, 147-48; material culture, 73; non-human, 114, 145; relief, 9; resources, 17, 53, 133, 146; settlement, 86; stories, 27-28, 41
human rights, ix, x, 7, 39, 46, 78, 85, 87, 134, 139
Hunt, D. Bradford, 142
Hurricane Sandy, 46, 164

ICA. *See* International Council of Archives
ICCROM. *See* International Centre for the Study of the Preservation and Restoration of Cultural Property
ICOFOM. *See* International Committee for Museology
ICOM-CC Joint Commitment for Climate Action in Cultural Heritage, 152
ICOM. *See* International Council of Museums
ICOM Define. *See* Standing Committee for the Museum Definition
ICOMOS. *See* International Council of Monuments and Sites
ICOM-US. *See* United States Committee, International Council of Museums
ICSC. *See* International Coalition of Sites of Conscience
identity, 4, 28, 32, 43-44, 52, 71, 86, 93, 95, 97, 103, 160
ideology, 47, 66, 97-98
IED. *See* International Energy Agency

museum(s), ix, x, xiii, 4, 18, 43, 77,
84, 121–28, 151–52; 21st century,
159–68; accountability of, 126–28;
administration, 51; "bad-news," 47;
community, ix; definition, x, xi, xiii, xiv,
xvi, 10, 18, 21, 33, 36, 43, 47, 51, 83,
114; educational, missions, 165–66;
empowered, 6; encyclopedic, 22, 86;
ethics, 36; ethnic-specific, 5, 22; field,
xiii; future of, ix, xv; of the future, x;
historic, 47; holistic, x; as influencers,
103–5, 113–18; leaders, xii, 36;
meaning of, ix; memory, 47; missions
of, 123–25; orthodoxies, 65; physical
space of, 164–65; as places of healing
and reflection, 161; practice, 35, 55;
primary function of, ix; prioritizing
people at, 122–23; professionals, xii;
purpose of, xiv, 63, 125–26; redefining,
128; role in social justice, 160–61;
science, 32, 162–63; sector, 19; in
social and environmental well-being
and change, 153–54; society serving,
x; standards, 36; state-run, 45; and
sustainability, 131–35; as temple,
51; today, x; trust, xi; universal, 86;
workers, 36
Museum Definition, Prospects and
Potentials (MDPP), 10–11, 103, 114–16;
Standing Committee, 115
Museum International, 115
Museum of Contemporary Art Detroit
(MOCAD), 162
Museum of Free Derry, 38, 39
Museum of Freedom. *See* Museum of
Maidan
"Museum of the Future," 142
Museum of Maidan (Museum of
Freedom), 46
Museum of Nevis History, 88
Museum of Unnatural History, 96
Museum Van Loon, 61
Museum Workers Relief Fund, 37
Museum Workers Speak, 141
Museum of World Cultures, 61
"Museums and the Sustainable
Development Goals" (McGhie), 145

"Museums Are Finally Taking a Stand.
But Can They Find Their Footing?"
(Cotter), 126–27
Museums for a New Century, 111
Museums Mobilize, 123
"Museums of Ukraine and Euromaidan:
Learning to Be with the People," 46

Naeem, Dr. Asma, 93
narrative, 5, 28, 53, 68–69, 99, 117,
138; about Whites, 96; absent, 5; of
the city, 31; controlled, 59; cultural,
98; decolonizing, 69; dominant,
97; historic, 4, 59; historical,
59; inhumane, 96; new, 148–49;
single national, 44, 140; of social
significance, 70; transforming, 68–70;
uncommon, 92; of upper-class life, 82;
of White supremacy, 67
Nashville, 8
National AIDS Exhibition Consortium, 167
Nationally Determined Contribution
(NDC), 153
National Mall, 22
National Memorial to the Heavenly
Hundred and Revolution of Dignity
Museum (Maidan Museum), 47
National Museum of African American
History and Culture, 166
National Museum of Emerging Science
and Innovation (Miraikan), 163
National Museum of Natural History, 163
National Museum of Tanzania, 87
National Museum of the American Indian
(NMAI), 22
National Museums of Kenya (NMK), 88
National Museums of Liverpool, 47
National Public Housing Museum
(NPHM), 134, 137–42
Native, 16, 23; American(s), 16, 22, 138;
languages, xi; non-Native American,
138; repatriations, 64; spokespersons,
16; voice, 22
natural history, 32, 34, 37, 77, 80, 109;
museums, 34, 81; specimens, 77
Natural History Museums of Los Angeles,
124

society, 4, 7, 20–22, 28, 47, 60, 65, 81, 84–86, 88, 91, 105, 113, 145, 154, 159; American, 7, 111, 121; attitudes toward, 7; benefit of, 84; Bosnian and Herzegovinian, 40; civil, 45, 47, 109, 146; contemporary, 59; development of, 87; global, 147; impact, 116–18; international, 144; museums in, 63; needs of, 46; norms, 59; open, 53; pastoral, 88; pluralistic, 52, 111; reconciliation of, 29, 44; service to, 29, 44, 115; values in, 28, 32
sociology, 70
Solnit, Rebecca, 139
source community, 36
South Africa, 39; freedom, 87
Soviet, 28, 44; post-Soviet, 44, 46
Space Center Houston, 163
Speaking Out, 40
Spock, Michael, 107
Sri Lanka, 36
staff, 16, 35, 36; diversity of, 36, 81, 127, 141; laid off, 36; making TikToks, 40; professional, 11; safety for, 37, 127; training of, 37
stakeholder, 8–9, 16, 86, 110–11, 123, 142
Stamps, Marion, 140
Standing Committee for the Museum Definition (ICOM Define), xi, 116– 117
Statue of Liberty, 36
St. Kitts and Nevis, 88
storytelling, 12, 142
strategic planning, 6
structures, 4, 17, 66, 107
student, 161, 165; immigrant, 80; Northwestern, 161; protesters, 45; White scientists and, 79
subject, 15, 23, 35, 51, 54, 59, 81, 84
sustainability, ix, xv, 86, 104, 107, 114, 131, 145–48, 151–53, 160; debates about, 145; definition of, 145–46; ICOM, 143–49; future, 111; long-term, 121; measuring impacts of, 153; and museums, 131–35; pillars of, 143–44; role in solving wicked problems, 154–55
Sutton, Sarah, xiv, xv, 134, 151–55
Syria: conflict, 87

systemic racism, xiv, 17, 134, 142, 159, 161

Tea Plantation Workers Museum, 36
Terkel, Studs, 139
"The Future of Museums: Recover and Reimagine," x; International Museum Day, x
Thornton, Jim, 93
Thunberg, Greta, 147
TikTok, 40, 164
Tisdale, Rainey, 37
"tomorrow museum," 46
tour, 24, 38, 164
tradition/traditional, 17; artisans, 88; cultural, 66; dance, 41; Eurocentric, 52; museums, 123, 164
transactional to relational, 108
transformation, ix, x, xiii, 5, 23–24, 43, 62, 104, 144; of museums, 107; social, 29, 32–33
Transforming Our World: The 2030 Agenda for Sustainable Development (United Nations), 133
transparency, 5, 45, 60, 168
trauma, 28, 37, 39, 44, 96; collective, 37; individual, 37; informed practice, 37; post-conflict and post-disaster, 29, 44
Triennial, 9, 10, 11; Kyoto, 10; Milan, 9; Prague, 11
Tropenmuseum, 61
Trump, Donald, 7
trustees, 11, 91–93, 97
Tuol Sleng Genocide Museum, 35
Turkle, Sherry, 59
Turner, Caroline, 43
Tweets, 46

Ukraine, 28, 44, 45, 46, 47
Ukrainian Centre of Folk Culture. *See* Ivan Honchar Museum
Uncatalogued Museum, 45
UNESCO. *See* United Nations Educational, Scientific, and Cultural Organization
unilateralism, 24, 28
union (unions, unionization), 11, 31, 37; "a more perfect," 96
United for Biodiversity, 147

About the Contributors

George Henry Okello Abungu is an archaeologist and emeritus director-general of the National Museums of Kenya. He is the founding chairman of Africa 2009, the International Standing Committee on the Traffic in Illicit Antiquities, and the Centre for Heritage Development in Africa. He is the recipient of several awards, including the Ife Prize in Museology (2007), Distinction of Passeur du Patrimoine (2009), Lifetime Achievement in Defense of Art (2012), Chevalier de l'Ordre des Arts et des Lettres (2012), African World Heritage Fund Award (2016), and Ordre National du Lion Chevalier, Senegal (2018). He was vice president of International Council of Museums-US (ICOM-US), Kenya's representative to the UNESCO World Heritage Committee, and is currently a fellow of the Stellenbosch Institute for Advanced Study, Stellenbosch University. He is founding professor of heritage studies, University of Mauritius.

Christopher Bedford is the Dorothy Wagner Wallis Director of the Baltimore Museum of Art (BMA) and the tenth director to lead the museum, which is renowned for its outstanding collections of nineteenth-century, modern, and contemporary art. Recognized as an innovative and dynamic leader for building greater community engagement and creating programs of national and international impact, Bedford served as director of the Rose Art Museum at Brandeis University for four years prior to joining the BMA and was appointed as commissioner for the U.S. Pavilion for the 2017 Venice Biennale, which presented an exhibition of new work by American artist Mark Bradford. Previously, Bedford held the positions of chief curator and curator of exhibitions at the Wexner Center for the Arts at the Ohio State University (2008–2012), where he organized a nationally traveling exhibition of Bradford's work. He also served as assistant curator and curatorial assistant in the Department of Contemporary Art at the Los Angeles County Museum of Art (2006–2008) and as a consulting curator in the department of sculpture and decorative arts for the J. Paul Getty Museum (2006–2008). Born in Scotland and raised in the United States and the United Kingdom, Bedford has a BA from Oberlin College, received an MA in art history through the joint program at Case Western Reserve University and the Cleveland Museum of Art, and has studied in the doctoral programs in art history at the University of Southern California and the Courtauld Institute of Art at the University of London. Bedford is also a noted author and contributor to publications including *Art in America*, *Artforum*, and *Frieze*, among others. He is currently a trustee of Art + Practice, Greater Baltimore Cultural Alliance, and Maryland Citizens for the Arts.

Bruno Brulon Soares is a museologist and anthropologist based in Brazil, professor of museology at the Federal University of the State of Rio de Janeiro (UNIRIO), and professor in the Post-Graduate Program in Museology and Heritage (UNIRIO/MAST). He coordinates the laboratory of experimental museology at this university, working closely with community-based museums and with several projects at the grassroots level involving cultural heritage and museums. Currently he is chair of the ICOM International Committee for Museology (ICOFOM) and cochair of the Standing Committee for the Museum Definition (ICOM Define). He is the author and editor of several publications on museology and heritage, including the series of books "Decolonising Museology" (ICOFOM/ICOM). His research currently focuses on museum decolonization, community action, and the political uses of museums and cultural heritage.

Doctor of art history with national and international experience, **Lauran Bonilla-Merchav** is a lecturer, researcher, curator, and consultant of art, culture, museums, and heritage. Currently she is adjunct professor of art history in the School of Plastic Arts at the University of Costa Rica. She also teaches humanities and cultural tourism courses at the National University of Costa Rica. She has published on modern and contemporary Costa Rican art, as well as on topics of museology. Currently, she is treasurer of the Costa Rican Committee of the International Council of Museums (ICOM Costa Rica), having served as chair from 2013 to 2019 as well as treasurer of the Regional Alliance of ICOM LAC (Latin America and the Caribbean). She currently cochairs the ICOM Standing Committee for the Museum Definition (ICOM Define), which is undertaking a participatory process of consultation to reach a proposal for the new museum definition in 2022.

Lonnie G. Bunch III is the fourteenth secretary of the Smithsonian. He assumed his position in June 2019 and oversees nineteen museums, twenty-one libraries, the National Zoo, numerous research centers, and several education units and centers. Previously, Bunch was founding director of the Smithsonian's National Museum of African American History and Culture. When he started as director in July 2005, he had one staff member, no collections, no funding, and no site for a museum. Bunch transformed a vision into reality. The museum has had more than seven million visitors since it opened in September 2016 and has compiled a collection of nearly forty thousand objects. Before his appointment as director of the museum, Bunch served as the president of the Chicago Historical Society (2001–2005).

A widely published author, Bunch has written on topics ranging from the Black military experience, the American presidency, and all-Black towns in the American West to diversity in museum management and the impact of funding and politics on American museums. His most recent book, *A Fool's Errand: Creating the National Museum of African American History and Culture in the Age of Bush, Obama, and Trump*, chronicles the making of the museum that would become one of the most popular destinations in Washington.

Bunch has previously worked at the Smithsonian, holding several positions at its National Museum of American History from 1989 to 2000, where he oversaw the curatorial and collections staff that developed a major permanent exhibition on the American presidency. Born in Belleville, New Jersey, Bunch has held numerous teaching positions across the country, including at American University and George Washington University, both in Washington, D.C., and the University of Massachusetts in Dartmouth.

Among his many awards, he was appointed by President George W. Bush to the Committee for the Preservation of the White House in 2002 and reappointed by President Barack Obama in 2010. In 2019, he was awarded the Freedom Medal, one of the Four Freedom Awards from the Roosevelt Institute, for his contribution to American culture as a historian and storyteller; the W. E. B. Du Bois Medal from the Hutchins Center at Harvard University; and the National Equal Justice Award from the NAACP's Legal Defense Fund. Bunch received his undergraduate and graduate degrees from American University.

A native of Sprott, Alabama, **William Underwood Eiland** is director of the Georgia Museum of Art at the University of Georgia. He has a doctoral degree from the University of Virginia and has written, edited, and contributed to more than sixty publications. He has served on the boards of the American Alliance of Museums (AAM), the Southeastern Museums Conference, and the Georgia Association of Museums and Galleries; was a trustee of the Association of Art Museum Directors (AAMD), a chairman of the National Endowment for the Arts' Arts and Artifacts Indemnity Advisory Panel, and a vice chair of AAM's Accreditation Commission. Since 2013 he has been a trustee of the International Council of Museums. In 2013, Eiland received the American Alliance of Museums Distinguished Service Award in recognition of his contributions to the field on a national level. Most recently, in October 2017, he received the Governor's Award for the Arts & Humanities.

Elaine Heumann Gurian has worked in the museum field since 1968, first as a community activist, then as a director of museum education, and subsequently a professional deputy director for institutions dedicated to social justice and in the process of transforming themselves to address and embrace formerly marginalized groups. Starting in 1993, she has been a senior consultant to many government institutions worldwide dedicated to presenting a more fulsome and complex portrait of their history and people. Throughout her entire career, Gurian has been a teacher, writer, and mentor to community-based activist students and practitioners within the heritage field. Her work continues as an elder with the publication of her book *Centering the Museum: Writings for the Post-Covid Age* in 2021.

Lyndel King was director and chief curator at the Weisman Art Museum at the University of Minnesota from 1981 to 2021. She also was an adjunct professor in art history and professor of museum studies. Prior to the Weisman, King worked for Control Data Corporation and the National Gallery of Art in Washington, D.C., as well as had several jobs in an earlier career as a chemist and virologist. King grew up in rural western Kansas. She earned a BA in microbiology from the University of Kansas and a PhD in art history from the University of Minnesota.

King led fund-raising at the Weisman, implemented the design and construction of a new art museum building, and oversaw the selection of Frank O. Gehry as the architect. The new facility opened in 1993. She led successful fund-raising to work again with Gehry on an expansion of the museum that opened in 2011.

She has served on the boards of the Association of Art Museum Directors (AAMD), the American Alliance of Museums (AAM), the International Council of Museums-US (ICOM-US), the International Committee on University Museums and Collections, the American Institute of Architects-Minnesota, the Hill Museum and Manuscript Library, the Minnesota Center for Book Arts, the College of Visual Arts, and the Schubert Club, plus several other community-based arts organizations. She helped write *Professional Practices for Art Museums*, published by the AAMD, and has contributed to several other publications on museum management. In 2021, she was honored by the AAM with its Award for Distinguished Service to Museums.

King has been a professional external reviewer for many museums, as well as for the National Endowment for the Arts, the National Endowment for the Humanities, and the Institute for Museum and Library Services. She received an outstanding service award from the AAM for work as a peer reviewer and has received several awards from the American Association of Architects Minnesota for her contribution to design through her work at the Weisman. She presents international seminars on museum management and branding.

In her retirement, she is working on a book on the history and development of academic museums in the United States and Europe as well as continuing to participate actively on the boards of several arts organizations.

Danielle Kuijten holds a master's degree in museology from the Reinwardt Academy/Amsterdam University of the Arts. She is acting director and cocurator at Imagine IC, a pioneer in the field of contemporary heritage practices. Recent projects she has produced there were on topics of resistance, gender, and slavery. At Imagine IC she also heads the co-collection lab, which researches a variety of collecting/collection questions, such as how to work with shared authority and use democratizing heritage practices. As a freelancer she is active in the heritage field under the name Heritage Concepting. Her main focus is on participatory collecting methods, contemporary collecting, action curating, and reflective practice. Kuijten has been an active member of ICOM's International Committee for Collecting (COMCOL) and, since 2019, has served as its chair.

Lisa Yun Lee is a cultural activist and the executive director of the National Public Housing Museum. She is also an associate professor in art history and gender and women's studies at the University of Illinois at Chicago, teaching faculty with the Prison Neighborhood Art + Education Project, and a member of the Chicago Torture Justice Memorials. She has published books and articles about aesthetics and politics, public art, and the potential of museums as radical sites of resistance and for participatory democracy. Lee served as a cochair of Mayor Lori Lightfoot's Arts & Culture Transition Team and on the board of the American Alliance of Museums (AAM). She is currently a board member of the Field Foundation, the Illinois State Museum, 3Arts, and on the mayor's Committee for Monuments, Memorials, and Historical Reckoning. Lee received a BA from Bryn Mawr College and a PhD from Duke University.

Tom Loughman is a global arts professional with experience primarily in art museums. A trusted voice and passionate advocate for the museum field, his outreach and stewardship are well known in America and abroad. He has served since 2017 as cochair of the United States National Committee of the International Council of Museums. His scholarship on Early Modern Italian art, cultural patronage, and urbanism led to a distinguished curatorial career with art museums. He has served in executive roles at the Clark Art Institute in Williamstown, Massachusetts, and the Wadsworth Atheneum Museum of Art in Hartford, Connecticut. From 2016 to 2021 he was director and CEO of the Wadsworth Atheneum Museum of Art.

Kelly McKinley is CEO of the Bay Area Discovery Museum, a children's museum at the foot of the Golden Gate Bridge in Sausalito, California. She previously served as deputy director of the Oakland Museum of California, where she oversaw collections, conservation, curatorial, interpretation, exhibition design and production, and evaluation and visitor research. Other professional roles have included executive director of education and public programming at the Art Gallery of Ontario in Toronto and senior roles at Bruce Mau Design in Toronto and the Museum of Contemporary Art San Diego. McKinley has lectured internationally on museum leadership and taught in the graduate museum studies programs at the University Toronto, Bank Street College in

New York, and the graduate curatorial studies and criticism program at the Ontario College of Art and Design. She serves on the board of the American Alliance of Museums (AAM) and previously served on the editorial board of *Curator: The Museum Journal* and the boards of the Museum Education Roundtable and EdCom, the AAM professional network for museum educators.

Linda Norris is senior specialist, methodology and practice, at the International Coalition of Sites of Conscience (ICSC). She facilitates connections and builds the capacity of members and other organizations in the work of using the past to create a more just future. ICSC is the only global network of historic sites, museums, and memory initiatives that connects past struggles to today's movements for human rights.

At the Coalition, Norris has spearheaded projects such as the reinterpretation of Maison des Esclaves, Africa's first World Heritage Site; the community-based development of public art prototypes by Indigenous artists in Tulsa, Oklahoma; and body-mapping training for the War Childhood Museum in Bosnia and Herzegovina. As coauthor of *Creativity in Museum Practice*, Norris is an international thought leader in facilitating conversation and action surrounding the ways creativity can transform museums, shape more compelling narratives, and create deeper, more inclusive community connections. She has also written for publications such as *Museum*, *Exhibitionist*, and *History News*.

Norris holds an MA in history museum studies from the Cooperstown Graduate Program and an AB from Cornell University. She was a U.S. Fulbright Scholar to Ukraine in 2009 and continues her involvement with the Ukrainian cultural sector. Before joining ICSC in 2017, Norris was an independent museum and heritage consultant, working on interpretive projects and capacity-building efforts with museum colleagues throughout the United States, as well as in Canada, Ukraine, Romania, Albania, and the Baltics. Norris is also an adjunct instructor in the Johns Hopkins University Museum and Cultural Heritage Programs and blogs regularly at *The Uncataloged Museum*.

She represents ICSC in international museum and heritage contexts. In 2019, she presented sessions at ICOM Kyoto and has been featured at conferences in locations such as Estonia, Ukraine, Sierra Leone, and Turkey. She appeared on the *Museopunks* podcast episode "A New Definition of Museum?" and facilitates webinars for ICSC on a wide variety of topics.

Diana Pardue is currently chair of ICOM's International Committee, Disaster Resilient Museums Committee (DRMC), and a member of the Standing Committee for the Museum Definition (ICOM Define) and of the Working Group on Sustainability. She is a former member of ICOM's Executive Board, former cochair of the International Council of Museums-US (ICOM-US), and former chair of the International Committee of Architecture and Museum Techniques (ICAMT). Pardue works at the Statue of Liberty National Monument and Ellis

Island as director of museum programs. She manages the museum collection, exhibits, media, research library, and oral history programs. In addition to working with ICOM museums, she has worked with other organizations internationally in the development and programming of migration museums.

Since 2015, **Anne Pasternak** has served as the Shelby White and Leon Levy Director of the Brooklyn Museum, one of the oldest and largest fine arts institutions in the nation. For more than thirty years, Pasternak has devoted her career to engaging broad audiences with the limitless power of art to move, motivate, and inspire. As a staunch advocate for the civic and democratic roles our cultural and educational institutions can play, she is committed to projects that demonstrate the crucial links between art and social justice.

During her time at the Brooklyn Museum, Pasternak has focused on strengthening the museum as a center for the visual arts that is courageous, pioneering, and global. Through her leadership, Anne has expanded exhibitions, educational and public programs, and fostered special exhibitions, including *The Legacy of Lynching: Confronting Racial Terror in America*; *We Wanted a Revolution: Black Radical Women, 1965–85*; *Georgia O'Keeffe: Living Modern*; *Soul of a Nation: Art in the Age of Black Power*; and *Frida Kahlo: Appearances Can Be Deceiving*. These initiatives are building the foundations for the Brooklyn Museum's new Strategic Plan, to further the museum's mission to create inspiring encounters with art and engage audiences on the issues of today.

Prior to joining the Brooklyn Museum, Pasternak served for two decades as president and artistic director of Creative Time, where she initiated projects that gave artists opportunities to respond to political and environmental challenges while also expanding their practice and work globally. She collaborated with hundreds of artists, including Nick Cave, Paul Chan, Jenny Holzer, and Kara Walker, commissioning and presenting works that ranged from sculptural installations in Grand Central Terminal's Vanderbilt Hall to skywriting over Manhattan, as well as Tribute in Light, the twin beacons of light that illuminated the sky above the former World Trade Center site and continue to be presented on the anniversaries of 9/11.

Ihor Poshyvailo is a general director of the National Memorial to the Heavenly Hundred Heroes and Revolution of Dignity Museum (Maidan Museum) in Kyiv. He is a vice chair of the International Council of Museums Disaster Risk Management Committee (ICOM-DRMC) and a member of the International Committee of Memorial Museums in Remembrance of the Victims of Public Crimes (ICMEMO). Poshyvailo is ex-chairman of the Museum Council at the Ukrainian Ministry of Culture. He holds a PhD in history, was a Fulbright Scholar at the Smithsonian Institution, an international fellow at the DeVos Institute of Arts Management at the Kennedy Center, and a participant of the First Aid to Cultural Heritage in Times of Crisis training courses in the Netherlands, United

States, and Italy. He is the author of the award-winning book *Phenomenology of Pottery*, as well as numerous articles on arts and culture, cultural heritage preservation, interpretation in museums, cultural emergency management, and the presentation of conflicted history in museums. He is co-moderator and co-organizer of the museum management and disaster risk management workshops in Ukraine provided by the Fund for Arts and Culture in Central and Eastern Europe, the U.S. Embassy in Ukraine, the Smithsonian Institution, the Prince Claus Fund, and the International Centre for the Study of the Preservation and Restoration of Cultural Property (ICCROM).

Morien Rees is a museum adviser at Varanger Museum in Norway. Educated at the Welsh School of Architecture, he has worked as an architect in the United Kingdom and Norway. Since 1994 he has worked widely in the museum sector in Norway, developing museums and exhibition projects. At present, he is engaged in a feasibility study investigating the resiting of the Vardø Museum in a derelict gymnastics hall from 1934 and developing a symposium on femicide to be held on International Women's Day in 2022 at Steilneset, the site of Louise Bourgeois's memorial to the victims of seventeenth-century witchcraft trials in Northern Norway. He is chair of International Council of Museums-US (ICOM-US) Working Group on Sustainability.

As director of Parque Explora, Colombia's largest science museum, aquarium, and planetarium, **Andrés Roldán** works with his team on the creation of compelling and innovative learning environments and museums for science and cultural engagement. He also aims to "dilute" the museum's walls and take its influence to different territories and communities, providing educational strategies, community processes, and movable experiences that connect people through learning experiences. Roldán has vast experience in the conceptualization, design, and construction of exhibitions, as well as in the development of educational strategies. He also stands out for cultural planning, alliance building, fund-raising, and the management of interdisciplinary teams. As an active participant in Medellin's transformation, Roldán's work is based on the paradigm of socially committed museums. He believes the union between education, culture, urban planning, and architecture is vital for fostering sustainable community development and social justice.

Lisa Sasaki is interim director of the Smithsonian American Women's History Museum. Prior to this appointment, she was director of the Smithsonian Asian Pacific American Center, which brings Asian Pacific American stories to communities through innovative museum experiences. Sasaki has worked in the museum field for twenty-five years for organizations such as the Oakland Museum of California and the Japanese American National Museum. She also served as president of the Western Museums Association's board of directors and as a member of the American Alliance of Museums (AAM)'s Facing Change working group and of the Advisory Council for the Council of Jewish American Museums.

Sarah Sutton is principal of Sustainable Museums, a consultancy for cultural organizations pursuing climate action, and is the cultural sector lead for America Is All In, the U.S. subnational actors supporting the Paris Agreement. She is also grants manager for the Frankenthaler Climate Initiative, a grant program supporting energy efficiency and clean energy projects at visual arts institutions. She teaches in the Harvard University Extension School Museum Studies program and serves on the Climate Task Force for the American Psychological Association. Sutton is a coauthor of two editions of *The Green Museum* (as Sarah Brophy) and author of *Environmental Sustainability at Historic Sites & Museums*.

W. Richard West Jr. is president and CEO emeritus, ambassador, Native communities of the Autry Museum of the American West, which he directed from 2013 to 2021. West is also the founding director and director emeritus of the Smithsonian Institution's National Museum of the American Indian, where he served as director from 1990 to 2007. West has devoted his professional life and much of his personal life to working in the national and international museum communities and with American Indians on cultural, educational, legal, and governmental issues.

West practiced law at the Indian-owned Albuquerque law firm of Gover, Stetson, Williams & West, P.C. (1988–1990). He also was an associate attorney and then partner in the Washington, D.C., office of Fried, Frank, Harris, Shriver & Jacobson (1973–1988). He served as counsel to numerous American Indian tribes, communities, and organizations. In that capacity, he represented clients before federal, state, and tribal courts, various executive departments of the federal government, and Congress.

West's current board affiliations and memberships include the International Coalition of Sites of Conscience (2007–present); the Association of Tribal Archives, Libraries, and Museums (2015–present); the California Association of Museums (2019–present); the Denver Art Museum (2021–present); the UCLA Institute of Environment and Sustainability (2021–present); the Center for Large Landscape Conservation (2021–present); and the Albuquerque Museum Foundation (2021–present). He also has served on the boards of trustees of the Ford Foundation, Stanford University, and the Kaiser Family Foundation.

He served as chair of the board for the American Alliance of Museums (AAM) from 1998 to 2000. From 1992 to 1995 and 1997 to 1998, he served as member-at-large of AAM's board of directors and in 1995–1996 as vice chair of the board of directors. West was also a member-at-large (2004–2007) and vice president (2007–2010) of the International Council of Museums.

West, who grew up in Muskogee, Oklahoma, was born in San Bernardino, California, the son of an American Indian master artist, the late Walter Richard West Sr., and Maribelle McCrea West. He earned a bachelor's degree in American history magna cum laude in 1965 and graduated Phi Beta Kappa from the University of Redlands in California. He received a master's degree in American history from Harvard University in 1968. West graduated from the Stanford University School of Law with a doctor of jurisprudence degree in 1971, where he also was the recipient of the Hilmer Oehlmann Jr. Prize for excellence in legal writing and served as an editor and note editor of the *Stanford Law Review*.

West is a citizen of the Cheyenne and Arapaho Tribes in the state of Oklahoma. He is also a member of the Society of Southern Cheyenne Peace Chiefs. He is married to Mary Beth West, who retired from the U.S. Department of State in 2005. They have two adult children, Amy and Ben, and two grandchildren, Oliver and Finnian.

Christina Woods has twenty-seven years of experience working with underserved communities and individuals and serves the Duluth Art Institute (DAI) as its first Anishinaabe executive director. Currently, she serves on the City of Duluth Public Arts Commission, the State of Minnesota Capitol Arts Committee as the chair, and is a State of Minnesota CAAPB task force participant, and Past-Duluth League of Woman Voters as the president. Woods is an enrolled member of the Bois Forte Band of Chippewa and works closely with the Anishinaabe community as a leader and mentor. She also conducts trainings and workshops on equity, diversity, and inclusion, including the program she created for the DAI, Commission Your Bias. Woods's work in social justice brings a unique lens to the context of an arts organization. She is a 2019 AARP 50 Over 50 awardee in bias busting. She holds a bachelor's degree in elementary education and a master's degree in education in leadership. Woods is called upon locally, regionally, and nationally as an expert in decolonization, diversity, equity, and inclusion. She consults on these topics through her company, Diversity Consulting.

A top talent, brilliant administrator, and strategist, Woods's success includes a fourteen-year career teaching, ten years narrating and doing on-camera work for the national program *Native Report*, and twenty-five years writing curriculum and grants, fund-raising, and diversity/inclusion consulting. Woods brings an extensive range of nonprofit experience as a board member, executive director, and business leader. She lives in Duluth, Minnesota, with her acknowledged home in the Bois Forte Nation of northern Minnesota.

Tukufu Zuberi is the Lasry Family Professor of Race Relations and professor of sociology and Africana studies at the University of Pennsylvania. He is lead curator of the Africa Galleries at the Penn Museum. Zuberi's vision is dedicated to education.

He curated *Tides of Freedom: African Presence on the Delaware* at the Independence Seaport Museum (2013). Using four key moments in Philadelphia's history representing the themes of enslavement, emancipation, Jim Crow, and civil rights, *Tides of Freedom* urged visitors both to bear witness to a story central to Philadelphia and American history and to think about the meaning of "freedom" both historically and in today's world. His exhibition *Black Bodies in Propaganda: The Art of the War Poster* premiered at the University of Pennsylvania Museum of Archaeology and Anthropology (2013) and was presented at the Northwest African American Museum in Seattle (2016) and the Thomas Gilcrease Institute of American History and Art, Tulsa (2017). Zuberi curated the redesign of the Penn Museum's Africa Gallery, *AFRICA GALLERIES from Maker to Museum* (2019), for which he directed nine interstitials.

From 2003 to 2014, Zuberi was a host of the hit Public Broadcasting System (PBS) series *History Detectives*. *History Detectives* regularly presented the social history of American culture to the public. In 2014, Zuberi returned as host and coproducer of the PBS series *History Detectives: Special Investigations*. He is the writer and producer of *African Independence*, a feature-length documentary film that highlights the birth, realization, and problems confronted by the movement to win independence in Africa. *African Independence* was selected and featured at more than a dozen film festivals and was the recipient of various awards. Completed in 2020, his feature-length documentary on memory and precolonialism in Africa is titled *Before Things Fell Apart*. His most recent short documentary on African material culture in museums is titled *Decolonizing the Narrative: Africa Galleries from Maker to Museum* (2020). The first in a series of three short documentaries, *Decolonizing the Narrative* is a thirty-minute exploration of the debates about museums, reparations, restitution, and race.

Zuberi is the author of *Swing Low, Sweet Chariot: The Mortality Cost of Colonizing Liberia in the Nineteenth Century* (1995); *Thicker Than Blood: An Essay on How Racial Statistics Lie* (2001); *Más espeso que la sangre: La mentira del análisis estadístico según teorías biológicas de la raza* (2013); and *African Independence: How Africa Shapes the World* (2015). He has written more than seventy scholarly articles and edited or coedited eight volumes. These edited volumes include *White Logic, White Methods: Racism and Methodology* (with Eduardo Bonilla-Silva), which received the Oliver Cromwell Cox Book Award from the American Sociological Association. He has completed the manuscript *African Words and Memory* (forthcoming) and is completing the edited volume *Decolonizing the Narrative of the Penn Museum Africa Galleries*.

About the Editors

Kate Quinn believes that museums and the people in them have the power to make change in society. She has been working and teaching in the museum field for almost two decades. For fourteen years, until 2020, she served the University of Pennsylvania Museum of Archaeology and Anthropology (Penn Museum), where she was director of exhibitions and special projects. In her tenure at the Penn Museum, she established new col-

Kate Quinn

laborative models for exhibition and program creation, which resulted in more than one hundred exhibition and gallery projects and even more programming initiatives with regional, national, and international collaborators. In 2016 Quinn led the development of the public program series *The Public Classroom: Race and Science—The History, Use, and Abuse*, which brought international experts from multidisciplinary backgrounds to Philadelphia to discuss the historical misuse of science to inform the construct of "race" and its effect on society. She also organized many notable exhibitions, including *Cultures in the Crossfire: Stories from Syria and Iraq* (2017); *Native American Voices: The People—Here and Now* (2014); *Black Bodies in Propaganda: The Art of the War Poster* (2013); *Imagine Africa with the Penn Museum* (2010); and *Righteous Dopefiend: Homelessness, Poverty and Addiction in America* (2008), the Mexico and Central America Gallery (2019) and new Africa Galleries (2019). Prior to the Penn Museum, she held positions at the Delaware Art Museum and the Philadelphia Horticultural Society after a number of years working as a designer and artist for many theatrical and film productions. In 2020 Quinn was appointed executive director of the James A. Michener Art Museum in Doylestown, Pennsylvania. She is regularly consulted by nonprofit organizations and projects nationally and internationally.

Since 2017, Quinn has been on the board of directors for the United States Committee of the International Council of Museums (ICOM-US). In 2020, she and programming committee cochair Alejandra Peña Gutiérrez developed the webinar series *What Is a Museum? An Exploration in Six Parts* for ICOM-US, from which this publication stems. She is also a member of the Association of Art Museum Directors (AAMD), the American Association of State and Local History (AALSH), and the American Alliance of Museums (AAM).

Quinn is an alumnus of the Getty Leadership Institute for Museum Leaders (2014), an Affiliated Fellow with the American Academy in Rome (2012), and a consulting scholar for the University of Pennsylvania (2020). In 2018 she gave her first TEDx talk, On *Music, Museums, and Meaning-Making*, and has lectured at museum studies programs in Guatemala, China, Italy, the United Kingdom, and several universities in the Philadelphia region. She holds a BFA in theatrical design from Indiana University of Pennsylvania and an MFA from the University of the Arts, where she is currently a master lecturer in the museum studies program.

Alejandra Peña Gutiérrez

Alejandra Peña Gutiérrez is a certified architect from the Universidad Nacional Autónoma de México and has an art history master's degree from the Faculty of Philosophy and Literature of that university. She taught architecture at the bachelor's level at Universidad Nacional Autónoma de México, Universidad Anáhuac, Universidad Iberoamericana, and art history at the Center for Design, Cinema and Television in Mexico City.

Her experience in the field of museums started in 1992 as head of the Museography and Architecture Department of the Museo Nacional de San Carlos; later she was associate curator for the Museo de Arte Moderno, then deputy director at the Museo del Palacio de Bellas Artes, where later she became director. In 2001 she was appointed deputy director general of the Instituto Nacional de Bellas Artes (INBA) in Mexico.

She worked on the conception and development of the Center for Design, Cinema and Television, where she oversaw the academic coordination and later directed the continuing education program. She was executive assistant to the general director of INBA, then director of cultural promotion for the Directorate General of Educational and Cultural Collaboration of the Ministry of Foreign Affairs. From 2009 to 2012, she held the position of deputy director general of artistic heritage for INBA.

During the second half of 2012, she moved to Puerto Rico to work as deputy director at the Museo de Arte de Ponce and became executive director in

September 2013. In November 2021 she became director of the Weisman Art Museum of the University of Minnesota.

Peña Gutiérrez has been a member of AAMD since 2014; she is also a member of the Board of ICOM-US, where she cochairs the programming committee. Since 2020 she has also been a member of the Disaster Risk Management Standing Committee, which advises the executive board and advisory council of ICOM General.